THE DESERT HAWK

Barbara Hehner

THE DESERT HAWK

The True Story of J.F. "Stocky" Edwards, World War II Flying Ace

HarperTrophyCanada™
An imprint of HarperCollins Publishers Ltd

Published by HarperTrophyCanada™,
an imprint of HarperCollins Publishers Ltd

Front cover: Painting by J. F. Edwards.
Kittyhawk zeroes in–sweep over Knightsbridge
Kittyhawk Mk 1 Western Desert. Pilot J. F.
"Stocky" Edwards. 8 June 1942. Courtesy
of the artist.

First Edition

HarperTrophyCanada™ is a trademark of
HarperCollins Publishers

HarperCollins books may be purchased for
educational, business, or sales promotional
use through our Special Markets Department.

HarperCollins Publishers Ltd
2 Bloor Street East, 20th Floor
Toronto, Ontario, Canada
M4W 1A8

www.harpercollins.ca

Library and Archives Canada Cataloguing
in Publication

Hehner, Barbara, 1947–
The desert hawk : the true story of J. F.
"Stocky" Edwards, WW II flying ace /
Barbara Hehner.

ISBN-13: 978-0-00-639478-5
ISBN-10: 0-00-639478-7

1. Edwards, James F. (James Francis), 1921–
– Juvenile literature.
2. Canada. Royal Canadian Air Force –
Biography – Juvenile literature.
3. Fighter pilots – Canada – Biography –
Juvenile literature.
4. World War, 1939–1945 – Aerial
operations, Canadian – Juvenile literature.
I. Title.

UG626.2.E38H44 2005   j940.54'4971'092
C2005-902061-X

HC 9 8 7 6 5 4 3 2 1

Printed and bound in the United States

To my mother, Alice—
known in World War II as
Corporal "Mabbie" Mabbutt,
W4250, CWAC—
with love and admiration

CONTENTS

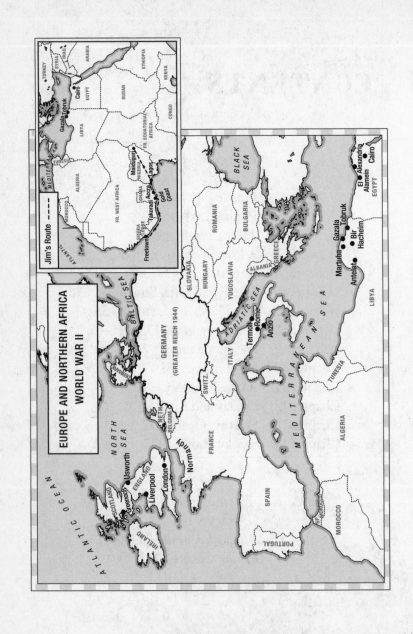

EUROPE AND NORTHERN AFRICA
WORLD WAR II

Jim's Route ------

PROLOGUE

The Bristol Bombay transport plane skimmed over the sand, just 50 feet above the North African desert. The rough vibrations of its engines made so much noise that the passengers on board—nine young pilots going to their first battle front—couldn't talk to one another.

Jim Edwards, like the others, sat strapped into an uncomfortable bucket seat, thinking his own thoughts. He was a twenty-year-old Canadian from Battleford, Saskatchewan. Just over a year ago, he'd been a high school student who'd never travelled more than 90 miles from home. Now he was in North Africa, headed for a place called Antelat. He couldn't imagine what this remote Royal Air Force base in the Libyan desert might look like. But he'd been told that the squadron he was joining had Hurricane fighter planes, and he'd been well trained to fly them. Jim felt a little nervous, but mostly he was eager to get into combat against the Luftwaffe, the German air force.

Checking his watch again, Jim saw that they'd been in the air for almost two hours. From what he'd been told, they should have been at their base by now. Just when he was wondering if the Bombay was lost over the vast, empty desert, Jim noticed that the pilot was throttling back the engines and he felt the wing flaps being lowered. Because the transport plane was already flying so low, it was on the ground in a couple of minutes.

When the Bombay had taxied to a halt, the pilots jumped out the fuselage door into billows of sand kicked up by their plane. The engines stopped, but the hazy air was still full of a loud, metallic chattering. At first, Jim couldn't quite figure it out. Just a few yards away from the plane he saw a large tent—probably the mess tent, he thought. But beyond that, he saw the source of the racket: teams of men were feeding bullets into two ack-acks (anti-aircraft guns) and firing them into the sky.

Jim's eyes followed the angle of the barrels upward, and he spotted two planes coming in low overhead. He stared open-mouthed. They were German bombers—Junkers 88s. He'd been trained to recognize them from drawings and diagrams, but here they were, the real thing. They headed off over a rise, and within seconds, a loud explosion made Jim jump. He could see clouds of sand and smoke rising in the air, but he couldn't see what the bombs were hitting.

"Don't stand about gawking—get in the tent!" Jim turned with a start and saw a man in the entrance to the mess tent, waving his arm frantically. He and the other new arrivals scrambled under cover just as two more explosions went off. Jim wondered how much protection a piece of flapping canvas was supposed to give them. There were a couple of long folding tables in the tent, but no one seemed to be diving underneath them.

Three of the men standing in the tent introduced themselves as pilots of 94 Squadron. Jim could hardly believe it. His first impression was that they were a sorry lot. Although his own clothes were sweaty and wrinkled after the flight, he was dressed in a proper summer uniform. Every one of the pilots was dressed differently, and one man was shirtless. They also needed shaves, and their shaggy hair was windblown and stiff with sand.

"Isn't there—um—something we should be doing?" one of the newcomers asked.

"Some of our pilots are already standing by, out on the airstrip," said one of the scruffy pilots. "If their planes aren't bombed to pieces."

"We can't take off, anyway," the second pilot chimed in glumly. "We've only got four Hurries left, and their wheels are stuck in the mud."

"It's all the rain we've had the last week," the third pilot explained. "Turns the airstrip into gumbo."

As quickly as it had begun, the attack was over. Everyone in the tent stepped outside to watch the two

PROLOGUE

German bombers climb into the clouds and disappear.

Jim had never imagined that his new squadron would be in such a desperate situation. What have I got myself into? he thought. How can we fight without planes?

Chapter 1

PRAIRIE BOY

James Francis Edwards was born on June 5, 1921, on a farm near Nokomis, Saskatchewan, about 80 miles east of Saskatoon. His grandfather Edwards had been a pioneer homesteader in the area.

Jim was the second child in a close-knit farm family; he had an older brother, Bernie, and two younger sisters, Dorothy and Jeanne. His parents, Wilfrid and Alice Edwards, struggled to make their quarter section of land prosper. When Jim was five and Bernie was seven, an early blast of wintry weather destroyed the Edwards's wheat crop before it could be harvested. To support his family, Jim's father took his horses and went to work for another farmer. In that farmer's stable, his horses caught sleeping sickness (equine encephalitis) and died.

That was the final blow. The Edwards family gave up

Alice Edwards in front of the farmhouse,
with Bernie and baby Jim on her lap.

on farming and moved to Battleford, Saskatchewan, a town of about 1,200 people, where Wilfrid studied to become an insurance agent. Although Bernie was eighteen months older than Jim, he hadn't been to school yet, because he'd been helping on the farm. The two boys started grade one together the next fall.

In Battleford, two more boys were born: Leo and Wilfrid. By the time Jim was ten, the Great Depression

Wilfrid Edwards with his children, in Battleford.
Back row, from left: Jim, Wilfrid, Dorothy.
Middle, in front of Wilfrid: young Wilfrid.
Front row, from left: Jeanne and Leo.

had brought hard times to Canada, and many people were out of work. The 1930s were especially tough years on the Prairies, where drought blew away topsoil and withered crops.

The Edwards children always had a roof over their heads, food to eat and shoes on their feet, but they had no luxuries. As the eldest, Jim and Bernie were expected to help out with chores. They chopped wood to feed the stove that heated the house. But the boys also did their share to provide for their family.

Every morning at 5:45 a.m., Jim and Bernie met the milk truck at the railway station and clambered aboard. The truck then slowly made its way up and down the still-dark streets of Battleford. The boys jumped down from the back of the truck and ran up to each house with bottles of milk. They left the bottles on the front porch and dashed back to reboard the truck before it got too far ahead of them. In summer, it took the boys about an hour and a half to deliver the milk. In winter, when temperatures plunged as low as $-40°F$, the milk was delivered by a slower sleigh, and delivery took about two hours. Each boy was paid for his work with two quarts of milk, which were very welcome in the Edwards home. Clutching the bottles in their mittened hands, Bernie and Jim ran home to gulp down a hot breakfast and then hurry off to school.

Jim never thought of the milk run as a hardship. He loved to be active, and his morning job still left him plenty of time for sports and games after school. Although he was smaller than many boys his age, he was fast and well coordinated and excelled at baseball and hockey. By the time he was twelve, he was playing on the town's baseball team with grown men.

To Jim, Battleford seemed like the perfect place to grow up. It was a town where people from different backgrounds mixed together and helped one another.

Jim had white friends and Metis friends; friends who were Catholics like him, and friends who were Protestants; friends whose fathers scraped together a living doing odd jobs, and friends whose fathers were bankers and doctors. Jim's parents taught him to respect people for their characters and abilities, not their social standing. Jim grew up believing that this was the way life should be.

Battleford lay between two rivers, the broad Saskatchewan and the narrower Battle. Jim loved to roam the prairie grasslands, where he could see the sky from one horizon to the other. Bushes and shrubs grew thickly in the gullies along the banks of the rivers, and Jim and Bernie knew every inch of them. They knew where the berries grew—saskatoon berries, blueberries, strawberries and pin cherries—and they brought them home in buckets so their mother could bake them into pies and make jam.

The riverbanks, and the grasslands between them, were also thick with game. Jim, like most Prairie boys of the time, learned how to hunt when he was very young. Hunting was the cheapest way to put fresh meat on the table. At six years old, he was already stalking small animals with a slingshot Bernie had made for him. When he was nine, his father taught him how to use a rifle, and by the time he was twelve, he was hunting birds—grouse, prairie chickens and ducks—with a shotgun.

Jim's father taught his sons how to "lead" birds on the wing. First of all, you have to pick out an individual bird—if you just fire at the flock, you won't hit anything. Furthermore, if you fire right at the bird, his father explained, you'll miss. Instead, you have to figure out the height, speed and direction of the bird and fire at where it is going, not where it is when you pull the trigger. If it's a windy day, you have to allow for that, too. With practice, Jim could make this mental calculation in a flash, and he seldom missed. He never had more than half a dozen shotgun shells, which were expensive, so he couldn't afford to waste them.

Jim's faithful hunting companion was his dog, Snap. Snap was black and white, a mixed-breed dog with a long coat like a spaniel's. One winter morning when the brothers were delivering the milk, the dog just appeared out of the dark and started to follow the truck. Jim brought him home, and the family tried to find out who he belonged to. No one in Battleford recognized the dog, and finally Jim was allowed to keep him. Snap was an enthusiastic hunting dog. He would sniff out partridge and chase them up into a tree, then sit at the foot and bark for Jim to come. He was also good at retrieving the birds that Jim shot down.

Two of Jim's closest friends were Metis boys, Paul and Edd Ballendine, who were also skilled hunters. They taught him how to creep soundlessly on his belly until he was within shooting distance of the ducks that gathered on a sandbar in the Saskatchewan River. They might spend an hour doing this, and Jim learned patience and the importance of timing.

Jim (on the right) playing hockey with Paul Ballendine (centre) and Edd Ballendine (left).

Even in a town of hunters, Jim was recognized as a good shot. He had keen eyesight and amazed his friends by reading the time off the large clock face in the post office tower when they were still a mile away from town.

Jim didn't spend all his time outdoors. He was a good student who took his studies seriously, and he also loved to read. His favourite book was *Tarzan*, which told of an Englishman raised by apes in Africa. Jim wanted to defy gravity like his hero, swinging through the jungle on long, thick vines. He was also impressed by how Tarzan saved himself from danger by using all his senses.

Jim had just one problem in his life—he suffered from terrible migraine headaches. Sometimes Bernie would have to help him home from school in the middle of the day. There was nothing for Jim to do except lie in the dark, with a cold cloth on his forehead, and wait for the headache to go away. He found that watching a movie might bring on a headache, so he went to very few, even though all his friends liked to go to Saturday matinees. As he got into his teens, he discovered that even the smallest sip of alcohol or one puff on a cigarette would trigger a migraine, so he vowed not to drink or smoke.

Both Jim and Bernie went to St. Thomas College rather than Battleford Collegiate. St. Thomas was a private Catholic boys' school run by the Oblate Fathers. Wilfrid used his small World War I pension to pay as much of the fees as he could manage, and the school waived the rest. St. Thomas gave the boys an excellent education, and it also had a championship hockey team. Jim quickly became one of its star players. The team was coached by Father Simon, a tall, fit man who had played professional hockey before becoming a priest. Jim played right wing, and he was very competitive, small but determined. He would cut in hard off the wing and go right to the net. Any opposing player in his path would freeze as Jim rushed straight at him, cut around him and deked the goalie. The St. Thomas College team won the interscholastic championship

Father Simon (front row, left) with the
St. Thomas College hockey team. Jim is the
second player from the left in the front row.

against other Battleford-area schools three years in a
row: 1937, 1938 and 1939. In the 1938–39 season, they
never lost a single game.

Father Simon was so impressed by his scrappy right
winger that he asked an old friend, Johnny Gottselig, to
come and have a look at Jim in action. Gottselig, who
played for the Chicago Blackhawks, arranged for Jim to
have a tryout with the team when he graduated from
high school the next year. Meanwhile, Gonzaga University in Spokane, Washington, offered Jim a hockey
scholarship. Jim had never expected that he would be
able to afford university, so this was a thrill. It was

exciting to have attracted the attention of the NHL, but he had made up his mind to accept Gonzaga's offer. The world was changing, however, and the course of Jim's life was about to change with it.

In the late 1930s, Jim and his family, like other Canadians, lived with the growing threat of war. The family listened to news broadcasts on the big radio in the living room, and they discussed them afterwards. There was conflict in many parts of the world: in Asia, where Japan was invading neighbouring countries; in North Africa, where Italy had conquered Ethiopia; and in Europe, where Germany was controlled by a Nazi dictator, Adolf Hitler. The Nazis were building up Germany's military might. They had already taken over Austria and part of Czechoslovakia.

In the peaceful farmlands of Saskatchewan, the threat seemed very far away. But Jim's parents and the older children understood that it could one day reach right into their home. If Britain was drawn into war in Europe, Canada, as part of the British Empire, would likely go to war, too. Jim's father had been a stretcher-bearer on World War I battlefields. Jim's mother, who was English, had lived through bombing raids by German Zeppelins when she was a young girl in London. Both parents had seen some of the suffering that war can cause. They hated the thought that the world might go to war again, just twenty years after the conflict people had called "the war to end all wars." They feared especially for their two oldest sons, who were almost old enough to fight.

Jim spent the summer of 1939 working on a dairy farm. By the end of August, he was looking forward to getting back to school and to a new hockey season. On Sunday, September 3, though, his family gathered around their radio with more serious matters on their minds. Britain had vowed to protect Poland, and two days earlier, Germany had invaded Poland. What would Britain do? With his family, Jim listened to the British prime minister announce that Britain was in a state of war with Germany. Later that afternoon, as the Edwards family remained close to their radio, they heard a message from King George VI:

In this grave hour, perhaps the most fateful in our history, I send to every household of my peoples, both at home and overseas, this message, spoken as if I were able to cross your threshold and speak to you myself. For the second time in the lives of most of us, we are at war. . . . I ask you to stand calm, firm and united in this time of trial. There may be dark days ahead . . . but we can only do the right as we see the right and . . . with God's help we shall prevail.

Canada followed up with its own declaration of war on September 10. By then, Jim and Bernie had started back to school, but no one wanted to talk about anything but the war. Most of the senior students were determined to enlist in the armed services. Bernie and Jim announced to their parents that they would join the air force, as many of their friends planned to do. Both boys still had another year of high school, and Jim was only eighteen. Wilfrid and Alice urged them to wait.

In fact, Bernie and Jim soon found out that the air force wouldn't take them without a high school diploma. Bernie, impatient to be part of the war effort, joined the army instead. But Jim was set on the air force, so he went back to St. Thomas College for one more year, as his parents wished. He was still a good student and a hockey star, but now he knew he wouldn't be going to Gonzaga any time soon. In the margins of his notebooks, he doodled fighter planes.

Chapter 2

JOINING UP

As soon as the school year ended in June 1940, Jim set off to join the RCAF. He put on his good suit and dress shoes, and stuffed his birth certificate and his report card into his pocket. The nearest RCAF recruiting office was in Saskatoon, 90 miles away along a gravel road. Jim planned to hitchhike to save money, and fortunately he soon got a lift that took him most of the way. He walked the last 10 miles.

Jim had enough money with him for supper and an inexpensive hotel room. The hotel he found was on the shabby side. The bathroom was down the hall, and he had to line up with the old men who lived in the hotel to use it. His room was tiny and its walls were thin. However, after his long walk in the summer sun, he had no trouble falling asleep.

The next morning, on his way to the recruiting

office, Jim spotted some salt and pepper shakers in the window of a 15¢ store. They were designed like two little ducks, and he knew his mother would like them. But buying them would leave him with little money. He hesitated, but then decided that he should have confidence in himself. If the air force accepted him, he'd be provided with room and board and wouldn't need much money. He bought the shaker set.

Jim spent all morning in the recruiting office, filling out forms and taking medical tests. One of the tests rated his lung power. He had to blow into a rubber tube to push a column of mercury up a glass cylinder and hold it there as long as possible. Jim also had to hold his breath for as long as he could. He held it for three and a half minutes—a record for the RCAF. His eyesight and reflexes were also rated excellent.

By the end of the interview and tests, Jim was feeling pretty confident about how well he'd done. The air force recruiter told him that he seemed like a fine applicant, but then he explained that the RCAF was not ready for him yet. They had to find more instructors and build more training centres before they could take any more recruits. Jim should go home and wait to be notified. He was completely unprepared for this, but he felt too embarrassed to tell the recruiting officer his problem.

It was too late in the day for Jim to start for home. He had only enough money for supper and one more night in the hotel; he didn't have anything left for travel or for breakfast. The next morning, with an empty stomach, he started walking home. This time, no one would stop to pick him up. The soles of his good shoes wore right through, and his feet became blistered. By dinner hour, he'd reached the town of Borden, about 40 miles north of Saskatoon. Jim went into a roadside restaurant and asked for a drink of water.

"You look pretty worn out, son," said the proprietor. "Can I get you a cup of coffee?" The man had a kind face, so Jim decided to tell him what had happened. Not only did the man serve him dinner, but he also lent Jim $3.75 for bus fare home to Battleford. Jim later repaid him the money.

After returning from Saskatoon, Jim went to work on a farm. Meanwhile, Gerry and Bill, two school friends who were a year older than he was, went to Saskatoon to take flying lessons at their own expense. One day, while they were out on a training flight, they stopped in for a visit. They landed their plane on the straight stretch of land beside the Canadian National Railway tracks. Jim eyed the plane enviously. He could not afford private flying lessons. He wondered if his turn with the air force would ever come.

Canada was, in fact, responding to the need for airmen as quickly as it could. When World War II broke out in 1939, Britain and its Commonwealth allies (including Canada, Australia and New Zealand) had very few combat aircraft. They had even fewer military pilots. In December 1939, these countries agreed to share in the British Commonwealth Air Training Plan (known as the BCATP)—an ambitious education program. Most of the training would take place in Canada, which had wide-open spaces, especially on the Prairies, and was far from the fighting. The first men who joined the RCAF were taught by former bush pilots, stunt pilots known as "barnstormers," crop-dusters and a few pilots who had fought in World War I, more than twenty years earlier. But far more instructors were needed. Most of the first trainees were sent into the war, but some of the best pilots were kept back in Canada to be instructors—usually to their great disappointment.

From May 1940, when its first training school opened, until 1945, the BCATP operated at more than 200 sites across Canada, from Stanley, Nova Scotia, to Boundary Bay, British Columbia. It had nearly 5,000 instructors and operated some 11,000 aircraft. At its peak in 1943, the BCATP was turning out 3,000 graduates a month. In all, the plan trained more than 130,000 aircrew in less than five years.

While Jim had still been studying for his final high school exams in May 1940, first Holland and Belgium and then France had fallen to the Germans. By August, as Jim toiled on the farm, Britain was under attack from the air. The Royal Air Force pilots—they were known as "the Few"—fought back so desperately that the Luftwaffe gave up the attempt to destroy Britain's air force and airfields. The German air force turned its attention instead to bombing British cities. The newspapers and the newsreels (shown before movies) were full of stories and pictures of London ablaze, and dazed and bleeding civilians, standing in front of the ruins of their homes.

Then, as the Edwards family had feared, the war came right into their home. Alice Edwards's parents, who still lived in London, were killed in a Luftwaffe

Jim (on the left) with his father and Bernie. Jim is wearing his summer air force uniform, and Bernie is wearing Jim's winter uniform.

bombing raid in September 1940. Jim, who had never had the chance to meet his grandparents, felt even more desperate to get overseas and fight.

A new school year began in September 1940, but Jim did not go on to higher studies. Instead, he continued working on the farm and waiting for the air force to get in touch with him. One day in October, he was driving a team of huge black Percheron horses that were pulling a hay rack. The farmer's wife hurried out to the fields from the farmhouse, to tell him his father was on the phone. Since his father never would have telephoned unless it was something important, Jim knew right away what the call must be about—his call-up notice had finally come.

He was to travel to the No. 2 Manning Depot in Brandon, Manitoba, to begin his training. This time he wouldn't have to worry about the cost of getting there. The RCAF had sent a rail warrant permitting him to take the train. And he wouldn't go hungry—he'd been sent meal tickets for the journey.

As the train headed east into Manitoba, Jim was already farther from home than he'd ever been, but he wasn't alone. He'd met some other young men on the train who were also on their way to Brandon, all of them excited to be called up at last. Their new military life began as soon as they stepped off the train. They were met by some sergeants who ordered them to line up, and they were marched about half a mile to the Manning Depot.

Before it was taken over by the air force, the Manning Depot had been an agricultural exhibition hall called the Cow Palace. There was still a strong animal tang to the place. Jim, who had always worked on farms, didn't mind it as much as some of the city boys. The first stop was a long row of barber chairs. The barbers, to amuse themselves, asked the new arrivals how they liked their hair cut. But as Jim quickly found out, everyone got the same cut—very short on the sides and back. Jim, who was proud of his thick brown hair, was relieved that at least a little length was left on the top.

Next the young men received their uniforms—black ankle-high boots, blue shirts, a blue woollen tunic and trousers, a wedge cap with a bright brass badge and a winter greatcoat—as well as a polishing kit and a sewing kit to keep their uniforms in first-class condition. Finally, each man got a blue canvas kit bag to carry all his gear. Jim and the others were in the air force now, although at the lowest possible rank: Aircraftsmen 2 or "Acey-deucies."

The men were assigned their bunks, either an upper or a lower. There were hundreds of bunks in rows, with only three feet between them. Lights had to be out at 10 p.m. The first night, Jim lay awake for a while in the darkness, listening to the mutters and restless shifting of the sleepers around him. He even heard some stifled sobs from homesick teenagers. Jim was only eighteen himself, but he was too excited about being in the air force to think about missing his family.

THE DESERT HAWK

The next couple of weeks were a blur of physical effort and military discipline. Jim and the other recruits marched and marched, and marched some more. They learned how to make their beds the military way, with the blankets tucked so tightly that a quarter dropped on the bed would bounce in the air. They learned to polish their buttons and their boots, and how to salute, and when. None of this had much to do with being a fighter pilot, as far as Jim could see. He was eager to move on to the next stage, Initial Training School. Instead, he and other recent arrivals were sent to do six weeks of guard duty at the Macdonald Bombing and Gunnery School, just outside of Brandon.

Almost every day, to keep physically fit and occupied, the Acey-deucies had to do a four- or five-mile route march. One day they heard noisy engines overhead and looked up to see several bright yellow Harvard training planes practising climbs and turns. Jim watched in awe as the air force pilots put their planes through their paces. Not only had he never been inside an airplane cockpit, but he had never even driven a car. Would he ever be able to master those manoeuvres himself?

Chapter 3

TAKING FLIGHT

"Your turn now, Edwards." The civilian flight instructor, Mr. Findlater, nodded at him encouragingly. Jim left the group of young pilots gathered at the edge of the airfield and followed his instructor. His parachute pack, hanging by canvas straps down his back, felt very strange. In fact, his whole outfit felt strange to him. It was a freezing morning in January 1941, three months after he had joined the air force. Jim was dressed in full flying gear: a bulky flight suit, leather helmet, fleece-lined boots and warm gloves. He clambered into the front seat of the plane, and his instructor got in behind him. Jim's brain was buzzing with all the terminology he had learned—ailerons, rudders, throttles, elevators. . . . His worst fear was that, after they took off, he wouldn't remember the names for the parts of the plane and what he was supposed to do with them.

Jim was going up in the air for the first time in his life. The plane was a bright yellow Tiger Moth, a single-engine biplane with a fabric-covered steel-and-wood frame and a wooden propeller. It had two enclosed cockpits and dual controls. The student sat in the front cockpit and the instructor sat in the rear. They communicated by shouting into a speaking tube called a Gosport, which ran between the cockpits.

Jim would never forget that first flight, the magic of leaving the ground and soaring. He had heard stories of instructors who tried hard to make their students sick with dives and spins. But Findlater didn't believe in nonsense like that. He saw it as his job to give his students confidence, and to give them control of the plane as soon as possible.

Jim was thrilled when Findlater turned over the controls to him and allowed him to fly the Tiger Moth in level flight. Then, with his instructor guiding him through the Gosport, he eased the control column (stick) to the left to bank the plane and make a shallow left turn. Suddenly what he had been taught made sense: the stick controlled the ailerons, hinged surfaces on the trailing edge of the wings. When the left aileron went down and the right aileron went up, the plane turned to the left. At the same time, he had to press his foot on the left rudder, which controlled the fin (vertical stabilizer) on the tail of the plane. Jim's fears about remembering the correct terms began to ease. A little while later, the instructor guided him through a shallow right turn.

It seemed to Jim that they were back on the ground in about fifteen minutes, but it had really been an hour. He couldn't wait for the next afternoon, when he could fly again.

Jim had waited many weeks for his first flight. After a few weeks at the Manning Depot and his stint on guard duty at the Bombing and Gunnery School, he'd been sent to No. 2 Initial Training School (ITS) in Regina. The ITS was housed in a former teachers' college, and it meant being back in a classroom again. He had studied Mathematics, Navigation, Wireless (radio) and Morse Code, Armaments, Theory of Flight, and other subjects. Most of the would-be airmen were like him, just out of high school, although some had a year or two of university.

In addition to the classes every morning, there were tough physical drills in the afternoon. A few of the students "washed out" at this point, which meant they were sent home. Jim hadn't had much fear of that, but he feared being shuffled into another training path. Some of the students would be selected for flight training, but others would be air gunners, wireless operators, or "observers" (navigators). The rumour went round: "Don't be *too* good in mathematics, or they'll make you a navigator." But Jim wasn't a believer in half measures. He studied for the highest marks he could get in every subject.

Evidently Jim's strategy worked, because he was sent on to No. 16 Elementary Flying Training School (EFTS) in Edmonton. Here he would finally learn how to pilot a plane. He was Leading Aircraftsman Edwards now, with a white felt "flash" on his wedge cap to show his higher rank. No. 16 EFTS in Edmonton had just opened. The barracks still smelled of fresh lumber. Jim liked everything about the school: mixing with a brand-new group of airmen, mostly from the Maritime provinces; the food, which he thought was plentiful and delicious; and above all, getting the chance to fly every day.

Although Jim was one of the quieter members of the class, he enjoyed the camaraderie, and he was on friendly terms with everyone. He was especially amused by the antics of an outgoing prankster named Bill Barker, whom he had first met at ITS. Bill had a trick he liked to play on the various drill corporals who marched them around. He'd go up to one of them, grab the top button on his uniform and ask, "Do you need this button?" If the corporal said yes, he'd quickly yank it off and hand it back, saying "Here it is!" If the corporal said no, the button would still come off. Bill also liked to stare up at the sky intently, pointing with his finger, until he had everyone else looking up, too. Of course, there was nothing to see.

After his first flight, Jim quickly gained confidence in the Tiger Moth. Each time they went up, his instructor, Findlater, turned over more and more of the flying to him. Over and over again, they practised takeoffs, turns and landings. Then one day, after Jim brought the plane in for a perfect landing, the instructor climbed out of the rear cockpit. "Okay, Edwards," he said. "It's all yours." Findlater grinned and added, "Bring it back in one piece."

Jim is elated after his first solo flight in a Tiger Moth.

This was it: Jim's first solo flight. And Findlater had arranged it so that he didn't have time to worry about it beforehand. By now he knew exactly what he should do. He took off into the wind, climbed to 1,000 feet crosswind, flew downwind and descended to 500 feet. Then he turned back into the wind, throttled back to slow the plane to landing speed and brought it in for a smooth landing. When Jim got out of the plane, he was grinning broadly. One of his friends grabbed a camera and captured the moment.

Jim came to love the Tiger Moth, and he flew it well. His instructors judged him to be fighter-pilot material, and he was ready to move on to the next stage of training: Service Flying Training School (SFTS). However, once again, the training school was under construction and not ready for the airmen. This was a big advantage for Jim and the other students in his class: it meant that they could get extra flying practice. Most EFTS graduates logged only about fifty hours in the air, but Jim got eighty-three. He and three other airmen who were keen to make the most of the extra time practised dogfighting (air battles) in Tiger Moths. They would take turns flying on each other's tails and manoeuvring to shake the other pilot off.

Jim moved on to No. 11 SFTS in Yorkton, Saskatchewan, in May 1941. The instructors here were all in the

*Jim in his flight suit at SFTS,
in front of a row of Harvard Trainers.*

RCAF. At Yorkton, Jim learned to fly a Harvard Trainer, which was much faster and more powerful than the Tiger Moth. The Harvard was also much trickier to fly. The Tiger Moth might forgive you for making an error, but the Harvard would not. The Harvard's wing or nose would often drop if you weren't alert and making corrections at all times.

Now Jim was learning formation flying, how to

recover from a stall and aerobatics—loops, rolls and spins. He learned to fly using only the dials and switches on his instrument panel, a necessary skill for flying in cloud or at night. Once again, Jim was lucky enough to get an extended training period, while the RCAF struggled to arrange transportation to the East Coast for the graduates pouring out of their schools. By June he had 102 hours in the air, seventeen of them at night. At the end of June he passed his final test, known as the Wings Test. As far as he knew, he had done very well.

But there was a shock for Jim at the end of SFTS— he found out that he would be getting his wings, but he wouldn't be getting the commission that would make him a pilot officer. Instead he would be what's called a non-commissioned officer, or NCO, with the rank of sergeant pilot. Bill Barker felt awkward about the situation, too. He and Jim had been buddies through all their air training. But Bill had been made an officer, with higher pay, a nicer uniform and many other privileges of rank, and his friend had not.

The Royal Air Force wanted to limit the number of officers, and the RCAF followed that lead. Instead of making all its pilots officers automatically when they graduated, the RCAF offered officers' commissions to only about half the class. Many Canadians involved with running the British Commonwealth Air Training Plan thought this was a mistake. They felt that since all fighter pilots would have the same responsibilities and would be taking the same risks, they should all be officers.

Supposedly, the students with the highest marks and the greatest flying ability were the ones chosen to be officers, but Jim felt that wasn't always true. He noticed that, in his course, anyone who had a sergeant as his flight instructor, as Jim had, was made a sergeant, while anyone who had an officer as his instructor was made an officer.

Jim on graduation day, getting his wings from Group Captain George Howsam.

Still, Jim felt proud and happy on June 27, 1941, just three weeks past his nineteenth birthday, when his wings were pinned on his chest. He simply made a promise to himself that he would earn officer's rank once he got into combat.

After getting his wings, Jim got ten days of embarkation leave, and he returned home to Battleford. He felt strange and unsettled. He had become used to military life and was eager to put his training to use. Bernie was already overseas, training in England, and most of Jim's friends weren't around any more, either. Battleford, like towns across Canada, now had few young men—most had departed to join the armed services.

His parents and his younger brothers and sisters were putting on a brave face, but sometimes there were silences at the dinner table. At those moments, it seemed everyone's thoughts had turned to the danger ahead. Only Snap seemed exactly the same. Jim's family told him that, for the more than eight months he had been away, Snap had gone outside to wait for him every day when school let out.

One sunny day, while he was still on leave, his mother packed Jim some sandwiches. He grabbed a rifle and went hunting with his dog. Later he sat on the river-bank with Snap and shared a sandwich. "I wish you could understand what I'm saying, old fella. I think it might be a long time before I can get back to you."

The next day, the whole family saw Jim off at the train station. Jim was to travel across the country, all the way to Halifax. This was the first leg of a journey that would take him to England, first to an Operational Training Unit (OTU) for some advanced flight training, and then into combat. The Edwards family had no idea when—or if—they would all be together again. As the train pulled out, Jim could see that his mother had tears in her eyes, but she managed a smile as she waved. His sister Dorothy held Snap back so he couldn't run after the train as it rolled out of the station.

Chapter 4

A LONG WAY
FROM HOME

For the first time, Jim was seeing just how big his country was. The train's route took him across the prairies of Saskatchewan and Manitoba, through the wild country of Northern Ontario, and down into the rolling farmlands of Southern Ontario and Quebec. The train went through some of Canada's biggest cities, and everywhere it stopped, more armed forces personnel crowded aboard.

As the train moved across the country, the men from Jim's class came aboard at the various hometowns where they had spent their leaves. Bill and the other new pilot officers made it clear that, until the train reached Halifax, everyone would pal around together, just as they always had.

Bill was as high-spirited as ever. At one stop, two of the pilots got off the train to buy snacks. But the nearest store was farther away than they expected. When the train was about to depart without them, Bill lay down on the tracks in front of the train and shouted that he wasn't moving until his friends returned. Just when the station master was threatening to call the police to remove him, the two men came running back, clutching the snacks. Completely out of breath, they scrambled aboard the train, and Bill followed, waving a cheerful farewell to the irate station master.

After four days on the train, Jim finally arrived in Halifax. The first thing that struck him was the strong odour of fish near the harbour, something he'd never smelled before. He was also seeing the ocean for the first time—or at least Bedford Basin, Halifax's inner harbour, which was crowded with over a hundred ships of all sizes.

The train ride had been the last chance for Jim and some of his friends to treat one another as equals. In Halifax, Bill Barker and the other officers, looking sharp in their new uniforms and flat hats, went off to better accommodations. The sergeants, including Jim, were directed to a large old stone building near the waterfront. Wharf rats scurried across the floors at night, keeping Jim awake. He threw his boots and anything else that was handy to shoo them away.

When the airmen boarded the *Ausonia*, the troop ship that would take them to England, it was more of the same. Officers like Bill Barker had cabins, while the sergeants were directed to the hold of the ship, where they slept on hammocks. The two groups ate in different dining rooms, and when Jim and Bill met now, Jim had to salute him. Jim realized that life in the air force was going to be very different from life in Battleford, where all kinds of people had mixed together as equals.

Jim left Halifax in the middle of July 1941, in a large convoy of ships guarded by corvettes and destroyers. Every ship kept watch for U-boats (German submarines) that might torpedo them at any hour of the day or night. As Jim lay in his swaying hammock far below the waterline, he thought that he'd have little chance to escape if the ship was hit. However, his convoy was one of the lucky ones. After a stop in Iceland, Jim reached the British Isles safely in early August.

His ship arrived in the harbour at Greenoch, Scotland, late at night, while Jim was still asleep. He and the others in their hammocks were awakened by a strong jolt. Then they heard a muffled explosion. There were further explosions, and Jim and the other NCOs wondered whether their ship was being torpedoed. They began to scramble into their clothes, thinking they might go down at any moment. When several members of the ship's crew arrived, the airmen demanded to know what was going on. The crewmen told them not to worry, but wouldn't give them any information about the explosions. Instead, to Jim's indignation, the crewmen tried to lead them in a sing-along to calm them down.

Only after they were on land were they told what had happened. The destroyers in their convoy had fired depth charges as they entered the harbour. This was to discourage any U-boats that might be trying to slip into the harbour behind them. It was done as a precaution every time an Allied convoy entered the harbour.

Jim was disgusted that he and the other men had not been told what was going on. Ignorance is a terrible thing when you might be in danger, he thought. And he vowed to himself that if he was ever in a position to lead men, he'd respect them and keep them informed.

The next day, the airmen were loaded on trains heading south to England. Jim's train was shunted onto a siding for a few hours to let other rail traffic through. Gazing out the window, he saw a grass airfield, a little bigger than a soccer field, not far from the rail line. As he watched in fascination, six RAF Spitfire fighter planes took off in formation. They headed south for the English Channel and the skies over France, where they would battle the Luftwaffe. Jim longed to fly a Spitfire himself, but that would be up to the air force.

The train was still on the siding when the Spitfires returned, about an hour and fifteen minutes later. Jim counted them and realized with a lurch in his stomach that now there were only four. The others hadn't made it back. The war suddenly seemed very close to him.

* * *

Jim's train took him all the way to Bournemouth, on the south coast of England. Hundreds of airmen who had trained in the BCATP were gathered there, waiting for their OTU assignments. The RAF could assign a pilot to one of three divisions: Coastal Command (which protected convoys and patrolled the English Channel and the North Sea), Bomber Command or Fighter Command. Jim desperately wanted to be in Fighter Command.

When he was assigned to No. 55 OTU at Usworth, near Newcastle, Jim was a little disappointed to learn that he would be flying Hurricanes and not Spitfires. Spitfires had sleeker lines than the humpbacked Hurricanes, and they flew faster. Still, he was going to be a fighter pilot in Fighter Command, and that was the important thing.

The Hurricanes at Jim's OTU were veterans of the Battle of Britain, fought the previous year. However, even these older models were much faster and more powerful than anything he had flown in Canada. The top airspeed of a Harvard Trainer was around 200 miles per hour, while a Hurricane could travel at well over 300 miles per hour. The instructors were veteran RAF pilots, on a break from combat.

At Usworth, Jim was once again among some of the pilots he had trained with in Saskatchewan. The RAF, though, strictly enforced the separation of NCOs and officers. The officers couldn't eat with their old friends in the sergeants' mess, and Jim couldn't enter the officers' mess. It made both sides feel uncomfortable.

However, everyone was equal in the air—all had to learn the same skills and face the same risks. Jim decided to focus on flying and preparing for the combat ahead. He practised formation flying with other aircraft, and very low-level flying, just over the treetops. After several weeks of soloing in the Hurricane, he was feeling confident in the air. But Jim was about to make his first serious mistake—and it could have killed him.

It was October 1, and Jim was taking off for his fifth flight of the day. The skies had been overcast all day, and the weather was worsening. He was flying with his instructor and another new pilot in a V-formation of three planes, called a "Vic." The instructor, in the lead plane, took them into a heavy cloud bank. As Jim struggled to stay with the lead plane in the murk, his engine cut out. He broke away from the formation and used his instruments, as he had been trained to do, to make his way down. When he broke out of the clouds, he was only 500 feet above the ground, with no time for anything but a forced landing.

Below Jim were farmers' fields, neatly divided by fences and hedgerows. They were only a few hundred yards long, but one of them would have to do. Jim didn't put his wheels down, because he'd been taught that on a rough surface his plane would probably flip over if he did. He quickly chose a field, barely cleared its fence and brought his Hurricane down in a belly landing. The plane skidded along on the grass for about 75 yards, then came to a stop before it hit the next fence.

Jim shut off all the switches. He sat there for a couple of minutes, until his heart stopped pounding, and then climbed out. He hiked to the nearest farmhouse, where the family welcomed him warmly. To Jim's surprise, they treated his sudden arrival out of the sky as an ordinary social call. Nobody mentioned the plane in their pasture, or the big black furrow it had dug across the grass. "We always enjoy visits from pilots," the farmer said. "I'll just put the kettle on for tea," his wife added. "And perhaps you'd like to ring your base?" After Jim telephoned his base to let them know where he was, he sat drinking tea with the family. They peppered him with questions about Canada.

A truck soon arrived with an air force ground crew. When they raised the plane, they found that it had only slight damage to one panel on its underside. Jim was reassured to learn that the plane would soon be flyable again. But on the truck ride back to his base, he had time to think about the accident, and he knew he'd made a blunder.

Hurricanes, unlike the planes he'd flown in Canada, had two fuel tanks. The Hurricanes flown at the OTU were old and battered, and their main fuel tanks were unreliable when the planes were taking off. So the pilots were taught to take off on the smaller reserve tank. Once they were in the air, the section leader would give the order: switch over to the main tank. Everyone would flip their switches. Jim was pretty sure that his instructor had never given the order. Still, he should have remembered it. He'd run out of fuel because he was flying on the reserve tank.

Jim returned to his base and wrote out an accident report without making any excuses for himself. Then he had to appear before the squadron leader, who was also the chief flying instructor. As Jim stood in front of his superior's desk, he felt very anxious. What if, because of the accident, he was told he couldn't be a fighter pilot? Fortunately, the squadron leader was an understanding man. "Looking at this in a positive light, Edwards, you've gained some valuable experience. Forced landings aren't part of the training we offer here," he said dryly. "However, now you know what it's like. You survived it, and fortunately, so did your kite."

Jim was greatly relieved, but he had another concern that was not so easily resolved. He thought that the "sprogs," as the instructors called the new pilots, were spending too much time on formation flying, and not enough on shooting. When they did get a chance to practise shooting, the sprogs were taken up two at a time in old bomber planes called Fairey Battles, which were armed with guns. Another Battle would fly alongside, towing a windsock known as a drogue on a long steel cable. The sprogs would take turns firing at the drogue.

Jim was pleased that, even on his first try, he managed to hit the drogue, and each time he practised, he did better. But many of the young pilots had never fired a gun before, and Jim noticed that some of them never hit the drogue at all. How would they survive when they got into combat? Because the old Battles were often out of service, Jim received less than three hours of gunnery practice during his six weeks with the OTU.

Whenever he got the chance, Jim would question veteran pilots about air fighting. Were the Messerschmitt 109s, the German fighter planes, as fast as Hurricanes and Spitfires? Were they easily recognizable in the sky when they were above you or below you? What was the best way to get on the tail of an Me-109? When the Me-109s were escorting bombers, what formations did they use?

Some pilots, weary from combat, had little to say to the sprogs. When Jim questioned one veteran, a young man with haunted eyes, he growled, "If you score a hit, don't follow the plane down to see your handiwork or finish him off. There'll be others on your tail, so just get the hell out of there. This war has already had too many dead fighter aces." Then he stalked away.

Other pilots, not so tightly wired, did their best to share their hard-won wisdom. "Make sure you keep a sharp lookout in every direction, and especially behind you. Never, never concentrate on just one spot ahead," one pilot told Jim. Another one advised him that if he ever found himself alone in the sky, he should never fly straight and level, which would make him an easy target. Jim listened intently to any advice he could get, knowing it might keep him alive.

There were no more training stages after the OTU. After that, a pilot was considered ready for combat. Once again, Jim felt that his future was being put on the air force roulette wheel. He was sent to another manning pool, this time in Liverpool, to await a posting to an operational (combat) unit. He had always imagined that he would be battling with the Luftwaffe over Europe. But instead, he would soon be headed to a place far more distant and into conditions far more extreme than he had ever imagined.

Chapter 5

INTO AFRICA

In Liverpool, Jim found the waiting hard. He didn't go out to pubs with his friends because he didn't drink and the smoky rooms might bring on a migraine headache.

He had been writing home regularly but had received no letters in return. He knew his family must be writing, but their mail had not caught up to him as he moved from one base to another. When he was still at the OTU at Usworth, he had found a nearby skating rink. He had gotten a little ice time, wearing borrowed skates, but he had never had time to put together a hockey game with some of the other Canadians. He had written home asking his mother to please send his skates. That was before he realized just how slow the mail was going to be.

Meanwhile, he was given a leave, and he travelled to London, where his mother's sister and her family lived.

A bombed street in London.

He was happy to be meeting his aunt and uncle and cousins for the first time. They ran a pub called the White Hart, in the East End of London. This was the area of the city that had been hardest hit by Luftwaffe bombers.

Jim was shocked to see that whole city blocks of houses had been reduced to rubble, including the street where his grandparents once lived. It made him sad to think that he would never meet these relatives he had heard so much about. But everyone he met knew someone who had been killed or injured, or had lost their home. Although the raids weren't as heavy now, the German bombers still came at night. Jim was amazed at how calmly Londoners listened to the rising and falling wails of the air-raid sirens and the explosions of bombs. Only when the bombs sounded as if they were falling in the next street did everyone go down into the air-raid shelter under the pub.

When Jim returned to Liverpool ten days later, he and some of the other pilots were immediately ordered to get injections for cholera and other diseases. Then they were sent to pick up a new uniform, which included a tan-coloured tunic, shorts and knee socks. Obviously they were going somewhere tropical. Jim thought perhaps it might be India, where Britain had many troops. The military was always very secretive about troop movements, to keep word from leaking out to the enemy. Only the higher-ranking officers ever knew where men were being sent. Jim and the other pilots were told only at the last minute that the ship they were boarding was headed for Africa.

The war in North Africa had barely entered Jim's mind before this; he had always expected to be at war in Europe. Yet in North Africa, the Allies were engaged in a desperate struggle, which they could not afford to lose. At stake was control of the Mediterranean Sea and the Suez Canal.

The sea, along with the canal that had been completed in the nineteenth century, allowed British shipping to reach the Far East in three weeks. Without this route, ships had to go around the southern tip of Africa, and the journey could take two months. In peacetime, the Mediterranean route had been important to the British Empire's wealth and power. In wartime, especially now that Japan had entered the war in the East, it was even more vital. The Allies did not believe they could win the war if they lost control of North Africa, because they would lose the sea route to the East.

Britain had very large military bases in Egypt, especially at Alexandria and Cairo. Italy, Germany's ally in the war, had occupied Libya, on the border with Egypt, for many years. In the fall of 1940, while the Germans were bombing England, the Italian army invaded Egypt. After pressing forward for a time, they stopped and dug in about 240 miles west of Alexandria.

In December, Allied forces attacked the Italians and routed them. But Germany quickly sent in Panzer divisions with tanks and elite veteran Luftwaffe airmen. From March 1941 into the winter of 1941–42, Allied air and land forces waged a desperate struggle with the Axis powers, as Germany and its allies were called. The battle lines see-sawed back and forth across the Western Desert of North Africa. Each side had its victories, but neither was able to push the other right out of the area. The British commanders called for reinforcements, including more planes and aircrews.

* * *

Once again, Jim was on board a ship in a convoy, this time heading for Africa. It was November 1941. On the early part of the voyage, the ships ran into a violent storm. As huge waves crashed over the deck, many of the passengers were wretchedly seasick. Jim found, to his surprise, that he was not. Along with the other air-crew on board, he took his turn standing ready at the ship's machine guns. Once again, though, his luck held. The convoy was not attacked.

Within a few days, they had reached calm tropical waters sparkling in the sun. Jim gazed in wonder at the colour of the sea, which was almost turquoise. The ship put in at the port of Freetown, Sierra Leone, where Britain had a naval base. Jim and another pilot ventured into the town to search for a place to buy fresh fruit or vegetables. Jim's senses were almost overwhelmed by his first encounter with West Africa, but he collected a few vivid impressions: the humble, makeshift houses, some with vultures sitting on the roofs; and the strong scent of limes from the many lime trees growing around Freetown.

The next day, Jim and some other pilots were put on a Sunderland Flying Boat. This was a transport plane that took off and landed on water, and could carry about thirty people. They headed 800 miles south to Takoradi, on the Gold Coast (now Ghana). At Takoradi, Jim saw for the first time the jungle of his childhood dreams, when he had read his favourite Tarzan book over and over. He wrote a letter home, trying to describe the people of the Gold Coast, the palm trees and the tropical heat. He hoped that it would someday reach his family.

After wartime food rationing in Britain, it was wonderful to eat pineapple and other fresh fruit in Takoradi. Less wonderful were the mosquitoes, which carried malaria. Jim had to take anti-malarial tablets, wear long pants tucked into his boots, and sleep with mosquito netting around his bed at night.

The port at Takoradi received shiploads of brand-new Hurricane IIb fighter planes from Britain, in pieces. Local crews assembled them into planes, and then air force pilots ferried them, in groups of five or six, across Africa to Cairo. By the flight route they used, this was a distance of about 3,000 miles. Jim was to be one of those pilots.

As always, he tried to prepare as well as he could. He practised flying the Hurricane IIbs, which were a newer model than those he had flown in England. He quickly found out that these planes did not have working radios. When he asked a senior officer about that, he was told that the radios wouldn't be made operational until the planes reached Cairo.

"Sir, how will we keep in contact in the air?" Jim asked.

With hand signals, he was told. But what if he got separated from the formation and became lost, and couldn't contact bases on the ground?

"You won't get lost," the officer replied. "Just follow the trail of wreckage on the ground."

Jim smiled uncertainly, hoping that was a joke. After his next question, though, he thought he might need a trail after all. When he asked for a map of the territory he would pass over, he was told there weren't any. The piece of paper Jim *was* given to carry didn't reassure him either. Written in several African languages, it offered a reward if the downed airman who carried it was not killed, but was instead turned over to the British.

Jim and six other Hurricane pilots set out from Takoradi, following a Blenheim bomber whose crew had flown the route many times. The skies were clear, to his relief, and he could easily keep track of the other planes. They flew at 12,000 feet, and from that height he had a panoramic view. Sometimes they were flying over grasslands, and sometimes over dark jungle. Jim thought that if he had to try a forced landing in such thick vegetation, he'd be a dead man.

Their first refuelling stop came at a base near Accra, still in the Gold Coast, just in time for lunch. Then the planes took to the air again, headed for Lagos, Nigeria. The pilots spent the night in tents and were on their way again at first light. The land below edged from grassland to open country that was dry and brown. Jim was looking forward to his first sight of real desert sand.

The squadron's next landing was to be at Maiduguri, near the border of Chad. But Jim's plane, which had never been flown any great distance before, turned out to have a dangerous flaw. As he came in for his landing, the plane dropped its port (left) wing and Jim was unable to control it. His Hurricane landed with the wing dragging, did a ground loop (spun around) and wrecked its undercarriage. After refuelling, the Blenheim and the other Hurricanes continued on with their journey, leaving Jim and his damaged plane behind.

Jim couldn't understand how the accident had happened, until the ground crew inspected the plane. The feeder line that ran from the fuel tank under the left wing to the Hurricane's engine wasn't working. That tank had remained full of fuel, while the tank under the other wing had been nearly empty, and so the plane had been unbalanced.

It could have been worse: Jim could have run out of fuel and been forced down far from help. Or the dragging wing could have caught fire. But he was dejected anyway. He had now pranged two planes, and he had never even seen a German fighter plane, much less been in combat. But that was about to change, very soon.

Chapter 6

THE HARD-LUCK SQUADRON

After his forced landing at Maiduguri, Jim hitched a ride on a flight back to Takoradi. Then he set out for Cairo again, this time successfully. The air force sent him by truck to the Kasfereet air base, about 120 miles south of Cairo, to wait for a squadron assignment.

Kasfereet was a huge, dusty tent city crowded with British and Commonwealth airmen. Jim had to smile when he stepped out of his tent each morning. As a schoolboy, he had never dreamed he would travel so far from home and see such wonders. If he looked in one direction, he could see the Sphinx and the Pyramids. If he turned his head, he was looking at almost a hundred new Hurricane fighter planes, more than he had ever seen before. All of them had been ferried from Takoradi by pilots like him. Also scattered around the airfield were dozens of Blenheim bombers and other planes. The planes were waiting for their turn in action—and so was Jim.

Meanwhile, he had the chance to take a closer look at the Pyramids. He passed on the chance to ride a camel, however, after deciding he didn't like the look in its eye.

Finally the day came when he and eight other pilots were ordered to report to 94 Squadron, at a remote desert base called Antelat, 650 miles west of Cairo. And there, at last, were the German planes he had waited so long to see—bombing the airfield as he arrived.

Jim soon learned why the veteran pilots of 94 Squadron were so glum: their squadron had taken a beating. The squadron had been fighting in the North African desert since October 1941. They had strafed (shot from the air) Italian and German ground targets such as transport vehicles and troops, and battled in the air with Messerschmitts. They had had some success. But by the time Jim and the other new pilots arrived in late January, the squadron was in a desperate state.

A few days earlier, several of their Hurricanes had been shot down. Over the past weeks, a number of their pilots had been killed, including the commanding officer of the squadron and another senior officer. They were leaderless, and they had only four planes left, all mired in mud. They were near the Allied front lines, and the supply lines that stretched eastward behind them had faltered. They were almost out of everything, including fuel and food. All they had to eat was bully beef (canned meat) and hardtack (dry, hard biscuits), which they shared with the newcomers.

Jim spent his first night with 94 Squadron in a shabby tent. It had been put up and taken down so many times as the squadron moved from one desert base to another that it was in tatters. He was still hungry after an unsatisfying supper, and he shivered in the cold of a desert night. But more unsettling events were to come before morning.

While it was still dark, everyone was awakened by British army trucks speeding eastward past the camp. As Jim scrambled out of his tent to see what was going on, he heard one of the truck drivers call out, "The front's been broken—we're moving back. Pack yourselves up and get out of here!"

The men of 94 Squadron struggled to tow their remaining Hurricanes to higher, dry ground. At dawn, four pilots took off in them, heading east. The rest of the men, including Jim, hitched rides in army trucks. It was a rattling, jolting journey across the desert. Jim kept eyeing the skies. What an inviting target they were, down here. He felt like a rabbit watching for a circling hawk. But the squadron came safely together again, far from the enemy's lines. Word came down from headquarters that 94 would no longer be a Hurricane squadron. Instead, the pilots would learn to fly new American fighter planes called Kittyhawks.

Kittyhawks, single-engine fighter bombers, were bigger, heavier and more ruggedly built than Hurricanes. They were well armed, with six .5-calibre (half an inch in diameter) machine guns, three in each wing. The Kittyhawks' main job would be to escort Allied bombers and protect them from attack, but they could drop bombs, too. They could also be used for strafing ground targets. However, compared with Hurricanes—and Messerschmitts—they were sluggish in a climb and slower in the air. Their controls required a very firm hand.

After trying them out, some pilots refused to take to the air again in a Kittyhawk. Instead, they asked to be transferred to squadrons that still flew Hurricanes. Jim, however, was determined to master the tricky plane. He soon discovered its strong points: the Kittyhawk could make a very tight turn, and it could perform steep, fast dives.

While they got used to the new planes, the squadron also received a new squadron leader, Ernest "Imshi" Mason, a legendary fighter ace. Soon after his arrival, he led a group of the most experienced pilots against the

German and Italian air base at Martuba, Libya. Jim stayed behind with the other newer pilots, to get more practice.

Unfortunately, Mason's raid was a disaster. The plan was to surprise the enemy and strafe their planes on the ground. However, one Me-109 was able to take off. This one plane, flown by a highly skilled German pilot named Otto Schulz, quickly shot down five of 94 Squadron's planes, killing their pilots, Imshi Mason among them. After he heard what happened, Jim believed that inexperience with the Kittyhawks had something to do with it. Even the veteran pilots had been flying this difficult plane for only a short time. But Jim felt that tactics were to blame as well. He was beginning to distrust the flight formations the RAF used. They took a lot of concentration but gave poor protection to the pilots.

From what Jim could gather, when they were attacked, the Kittyhawks had formed a defensive circle and been picked off one by one. He felt sure that it would be better to turn towards the enemy and confront him head-on. It would also make sense to fly in a more flexible formation that would allow the pilots to watch one another's tails. But he was only a lowly sergeant pilot who had never been in combat. So he kept his thoughts to himself and bided his time.

Yet another squadron leader, Ian MacDougall, arrived at 94 Squadron. He saw at once that the pilots needed more time to practise flying in the Kittyhawks. Jim was pleased that the new squadron leader also favoured the Finger Four flying formation, which the Luftwaffe fighter pilots had been using for a long time. This formation had the shape of a right hand with its fingers spread. The leader was ahead (at the tip of the second finger). Behind him and to the side, acting as his wingman and guarding him from behind, was the number two pilot (at the tip of the index finger). To the leader's other side and farther back was the number three pilot (at the tip of the ring finger). And behind him, as his wingman, was the number four pilot (at the tip of the little finger). Under attack, the four planes

The Finger Four formation.

could break into pairs, with each pilot of the pair watching out for the other. But even training could be deadly—94 lost one of its pilots when he crashed and was killed while trying to recover from a spin.

Jim had discovered that you had to have a very strong right arm to fly a Kittyhawk in a dive. It picked up speed very quickly, but unfortunately, it tried to roll to the right at the same time. When you pulled out of your dive, it would roll to the left if you weren't ready. Jim found that he could control this by correcting in mid-dive, but it wasn't easy. He could only keep the control stick in the middle—holding the plane steady—by bracing his right arm against the inside of his leg, which in turn was pressed up against the side of the cockpit. Meanwhile, his left hand had to be on the trim, a control that fine-tuned the plane's position.

Jim also worked on his shooting. The guns on a Kitty-hawk were fired by squeezing a trigger on the top of the control stick. The key to hitting enemy planes was, first, to get in as close as you could. And second, you had to understand deflection shooting. This meant firing ahead of the enemy plane, at where it was going, so your fire would hit it. Jim used the open spaces of the desert, far from enemy lines, to practise "shadow firing" by himself. Skimming low over the desert, he flew so that the plane's shadow on the desert floor was just off his wing tip. Then he turned towards the shadow so that it moved forward, and he could practise deflection shooting at it from different angles. If he calculated correctly, the bullets would hit the shadow on the desert floor, kicking up dust so he could see where they went.

Long ago, Jim's father had taught him how to shoot birds on the wing. Now, he knew, his father's teachings and his own quick judgment were going to be put to their hardest test.

Chapter 7

THE HAWK
OF MARTUBA

All the time that Jim had been training on the Kitty-hawk, British ground forces had been pulling back as the Germans advanced. Eventually, they reached Gazala, 30 miles west of Tobruk, on the coast of Libya. On a line stretching from Gazala to Bir Hacheim, where there was a fort defended by Free French forces who were their allies, the British army dug in. They were determined not to lose the vital port of Tobruk, which was only about 400 miles from Cairo. After their training period, 94 Squadron moved back up to the new front near Tobruk, at an airfield that had been bulldozed out of the sand.

On March 23, 1942, the desert skies were a clear, burning blue. The Kittyhawks were so hot from sitting in the sun that the airmen couldn't touch them without gloves. Jim was finally going on his first operational sortie (combat mission). Once again, the target was the German and Italian airfield at Martuba. Twelve planes each from two fighter squadrons—94 and 260—would escort twelve Boston light bombers from a South African bomber squadron. Jim would be number two man, flying behind a more experienced pilot named Jack Phillips.

As he climbed into his Kittyhawk, Jim's mouth was dry and his stomach seemed to be doing aerobatics. What if he did something stupid and let the others down? That was his biggest fear, far greater than the fear of getting killed. But as soon as he was in the cockpit readying the plane for takeoff, he felt steadier. He was too busy with all the checks and takeoff procedures to be afraid. The Kittyhawks took off together. If they had taken off one by one, the following planes would have faced blinding clouds of sand stirred up by the earlier ones, which would stall their engines.

Soon the planes of 94 Squadron rendezvoused with the other squadrons. Jim was now part of a large, orderly formation of planes advancing on Martuba. The bombers were in the middle, and the fighter planes were on both sides of them (close cover), above them (middle cover) and even higher above them (top cover). In this way, the bombers were protected from attacks that came from the sides or above. Jim, as one of the newer pilots, was flying close cover. This was usually the most sheltered position for a fighter plane, because Messerschmitts preferred to attack out of the sun, from above. All his senses went on high alert and he focused only on the mission.

The squadrons headed out to sea and flew parallel to the Mediterranean shore. As they neared the enemy air base, flying at about 8,000 feet, Jim looked down and ahead. He saw clouds of dust rising from the airfield a few miles away and thought to himself, Those are fighters taking off. But before he could think more about that, the bombers were turning inland and soon the formation was over the target. Jim needed all his concentration to stay close behind Phillips.

As the bombers went in, Jim saw first one, two and then three get hit by German flak (anti-aircraft fire). They fell in flames and crashed almost on the enemy air base. Jim saw no parachutes and assumed that all the men in those bombers had been lost. The other Bostons managed to drop their bombs, but a fourth one was shot down by flak.

Jim suddenly spotted three small planes coming up through the formation, and he realized they were the planes he had seen take off from the airfield. The bombers turned sharply to start the journey home, and their escort Kittyhawks started their turn, too. And then Jim saw one of the small planes—a Messerschmitt 109 fighter plane with black crosses on it—come up and do a wing-over. This was a manoeuvre that turned the plane 180 degrees and allowed it to level out right between Jim and his leader, Phillips. The Me-109 was now just ahead and to one side of his plane and almost on Phillips's tail. Jim instantly squeezed the trigger. As streams of bullets from his guns converged on the Messerschmitt, it exploded, with pieces of debris flying outward.

Jim had no time to think about what he'd just done—he was scanning the sky for Phillips, and not finding him. He looked back over his right shoulder and saw an aircraft diving on him. It was another Messerschmitt!

The enemy aircraft lowered its nose, which was armed with a cannon. With all his hunter's instincts, Jim knew that the Messerschmitt pilot had a perfect

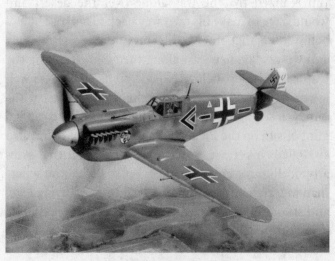

The Messerschmitt 109,
Jim's usual opponent in the desert.

angle on him. He felt a jolt of pure terror but again he reacted instantly. He pushed the control stick forward and then into the corner, so that his plane went into a steep spiral dive. The bright tracer bullets of the enemy plane skimmed over his cockpit.

Jim kept going down, pulling up only when he was almost on the desert floor. He swivelled his head, looking for the Messerschmitt, but it was nowhere to be seen. Why hadn't it followed him down? Maybe the pilot was out of ammunition.

In fact, Jim couldn't see any other planes. Not only had the Messerschmitts disappeared, but the Bostons and Kittyhawks, too. The sky was eerily empty. And Jim realized that he was alone over the desert and would have to make his own way back to his base.

Jim knew that the Mediterranean seacoast ran east and west, so he flew east along the coast, scanning the featureless desert below. Novice pilots, as he was well aware, had been known to fly right over their base without even seeing it. Some were lucky enough to catch a glint of sun on the Plexiglas canopy of a plane. Jim also swivelled his head constantly, checking the skies around him for enemy planes. Since he had no wingman to watch out for him, he tried to avoid flying level and straight, which would have made him an easy target. Fortunately, Jim finally spotted some bombers—Bostons that had just been on the raid—going in for a landing. His base was near the bomber base, and he realized with relief that he was almost there.

His return to base was so long overdue that there was no ground crew to greet him on the airfield. He unhooked his parachute and, hoisting it over his shoulder, started walking. Halfway to the operations tent, he was picked up by Squadron Leader MacDougall in a station wagon. "Get in!" he barked.

Jim could see that MacDougall was tense and upset. He was eager to tell him about the Messerschmitt he'd shot down, but he sensed that his commanding officer was in no mood to listen. Jim soon found out why. The bombers had gone in too low, and as Jim had seen, several were shot to pieces by anti-aircraft fire. In addition, three of 94's pilots had not returned, including Jack Phillips. Jim was supposed to stay with Phillips and had lost him, so he felt ashamed about that. But the Messerschmitt! That should count for something. And so Jim's mood swung back and forth for the whole ride, and he said nothing.

A few minutes after the men got back to the operations tent, the telephone rang. Jim could tell from MacDougall's side of the conversation that Phillips and another pilot were safe. They had run short of fuel and landed at an army base. As soon as they refuelled, they'd be back.

Even though one pilot was still unaccounted for (and later confirmed killed), MacDougall's mood lifted. He turned to Jim and said in a calmer voice, "Well, Edwards, what have you got to report?"

"Sir," Jim said, noticing with embarrassment that

his voice had become a rising squeak of excitement, "I shot down a Messerschmitt 109!"

Most fighter pilots, despite their training and bravery, never succeeded in destroying enemy aircraft in the air. To shoot one down on your first operational sortie was a rare feat. Within days, word of the young pilot's achievement had spread to other squadrons. A senior officer dubbed him "the Hawk of Martuba." Jim felt proud that he had done his duty, and that his practice had paid off. But he knew that he had been very lucky on that first mission. Not every Messerschmitt was going to be such easy prey.

Jim felt that he now understood what war was. It was facing someone who really was trying to kill you. He had never had an enemy in his life, but now he did. It was a shocking realization. If he didn't shoot at the Luftwaffe planes as quickly and accurately as he could, they would shoot down his squadron mates. And him.

Chapter 8

SURVIVING IN THE DESERT

Spring was the season of sandstorms in the desert. The British called them "khamsins," from the Arabic word for a hot desert wind. Jim had experienced many prairie blizzards but had never been through anything as unpleasant as a khamsin. It came as a billowing wall of sand, driven by a roaring wind. When it swept over the base, all planes were grounded. The sky was dark, even at midday. The men could get lost just going from their tents to the mess tent in the thick, swirling haze of the storm.

There was nothing for Jim and the others to do but huddle in their tents. Even there, the wind drove a fine dust right through the canvas. It coated them and all their belongings. Its bitter taste was in their mouths. Sometimes the wind was so strong that it broke their tent poles and brought their shelters down on them.

The khamsin also carried a strange electrical charge. Compasses spun helplessly and the men got unexpected shocks when they touched things.

Yet despite the sandstorms, and despite the constant danger of air combat, Jim quickly settled into the simple life of an RAF squadron in the desert. In fact, it suited him very well. The men couldn't unwind in the evening at a pub or a cinema, as they had in England—but then, Jim seldom went to pubs or movies. The desert squadrons paid little attention to the differences in rank that had made life difficult for Jim in England. In 94 Squadron, all the pilots—officers and sergeants—ate together in the officers' mess. (The ground staff, which included some officers, as well as the enlisted men and NCOs who looked after fuelling and repairing the planes, ate in another tent.)

There were few parades or inspections at the desert air bases, and everyone wore whatever was comfortable and practical. Each man dressed a little differently, with only a simple rank insignia sewn to his shirt. Jim often wore shorts, but he stuck to long pants for flying because they offered better protection if his plane caught fire. Most of the men wore suede desert boots, which protected their feet and ankles from thorny plants they called "camel scrub." But before they put their boots on in the morning, they turned them upside down to shake out any scorpions that might have crawled in during the night.

Everyone wore comfortable clothes.
Jim (front row, left end) is seen here with members of
260 Squadron. His friend Ron Cundy is beside him.

The desert did not hold the heat of the day once the
sun went down, and it became very cold at night.
Sleeping in his camp cot, Jim had a double blanket
underneath him and one on top, but he was never warm
enough. Later in the Desert War, he found a horsehide
cover that had been used to wrap a captured Heinkel
bomber's long-range fuel tank, and stretched that over
his cot. It kept the cold from seeping up into his bones,
and from then on he slept comfortably.

* * *

The desert squadrons were like nomads. Everything they had could be packed up quickly and moved by truck. The landing ground for a new desert air base would be levelled by an army crew, using a bulldozer. Then they'd clear the ground of stones. When the airfield was ready, the air force would fly in and land. Several squadrons, placed on opposite sides, would share the airfield. Each squadron had roughly twenty-four planes, but only twelve (called a flight) would be in the air at one time. This allowed time for the others to be fuelled and repaired. (An operation that needed more than twelve fighter planes would involve more than one squadron.)

Each squadron had a senior officer—a squadron leader—and about twenty-five to thirty pilots, as well as a skilled and dedicated ground crew of more than a hundred men who kept the planes in repair. The senior officer had a trailer that served as his quarters and his office. The rest of the men slept in tents, usually two to a tent, but sometimes six or more would share when they were short of tents. Their minor injuries and illnesses were taken care of by a medical officer (a doctor) and his orderlies (assistants). More serious cases would be transported back behind the lines to a hospital. The squadron even had a cook, who tried his best to make interesting meals out of the supplies they had. Everyone ate at long tables in the large mess tent.

All supplies, including food and water, had to be brought to the remote air bases by truck. Usually the squadron lived on canned fruits, vegetables and meat. Sometimes the men were stationed in an area where game was available, and Jim and some of the others would hunt gazelle and quail. Then they would enjoy fresh meat, but that was a rare treat.

Water arrived in a large tank on the back of a truck. The squadron stored it in metal cans. It was strictly rationed—one quart of water per man, per day, for all uses. Jim had a little more for drinking than some men, because at twenty he still wasn't shaving. There was usually enough water for him to brush his teeth and

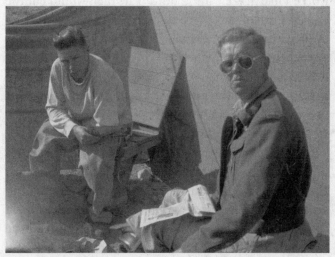

*On the bivvy: Jim (left) and a squadron mate
at Gar el Arid in the desert.*

wash his face, but a full bath was impossible. The squadron pilots were equipped with folding canvas basins that stood on wooden legs. Jim could put a little water in his and give himself a wash with a washcloth. Toilets were just as simple. The "bivvy" was a wooden box with a hole in it and a holding pot underneath. The men strung some canvas around it for privacy. Sometimes, Jim would just walk a little way out into the desert with a shovel and paper, dig a hole, use it and cover it over.

In the desert, the men's clothes became stiff with sweat and sand. But no water could be spared for laundry. Instead, they used gasoline to clean their clothes. It worked like dry-cleaning fluid. The men would cut the top off a can of gasoline and bunch up a jacket or a pair of pants until it fitted down inside the can. Next they swooshed the garment around in the gasoline until it was saturated. Then they either hung it to dry or spread it out on the sand. In the desert heat, the gasoline evaporated in about ten minutes, and once they were dry, the clothes were clean and odourless.

Even a light breeze would drive sand into the engines of the airplanes, so they wore out quickly. Worse, they could seize up in the air. Sand jammed their guns and scratched the Plexiglas canopies of the planes. Sand got into tents, into clothes and into hair. When Jim ate, he had the added crunch of sand in his teeth. If he rubbed his eye, he rubbed grit into it.

Still, it was a healthy life in many ways. Because the

desert was almost uninhabited and had extremes of hot and cold, there were no infectious diseases. Except at bases right on the coast, there were no flies or mosquitoes to pester the men. The climate also seemed to ease Jim's migraines. He had worried about how he would cope with his headaches, but he never had one while flying. Gradually they faded away entirely and never troubled him again.

For Jim, there was beauty in the desert. He had always liked a big sky. The sunsets could be magnificent, filling the western sky with red and violet. On nights with a full moon, the desert seemed to glow with a soft light. It was bright enough to read by. On a clear night with no moon, the thousands of brilliant stars looked close enough to touch.

Through the early spring of 1942, Jim's 94 Squadron and its sister RAF squadron, 260, kept up their efforts to slow the German advance. With each squadron providing one flight of twelve planes, they escorted bombers every second day or so, unless a sandstorm shut them down. Often the Messerschmitt pilots were already in the air, waiting for them, when they arrived at the target. They would swoop down out of the sun, attacking the top-cover Kittyhawks first.

Jim was still assigned to close cover, and he found it frustrating. The Messerschmitts rarely came close enough to him that he could take a shot at one. It was a little safer, but he wanted a chance to fire on the Luftwaffe planes. However, he did his duty, which was to stay in his assigned place in the formation.

On May 9, to the men's complete shock, 94 Squadron was ordered out of the desert and sent to a base far behind the lines. Their losses had been heavy, and headquarters felt they needed a breather. However, seven of the most effective pilots, including Jim, were transferred to 260 Squadron. Since this squadron had been carrying out operations with 94, it simply meant walking across the airfield.

Chapter 9

DESPERATE DAYS

Jim already knew some of the pilots at 260, and most of them knew him as well—at least by reputation. He had now flown sixteen operational sorties and was becoming recognized as a skilled fighter pilot. Now when the squadron escorted bombers, he flew top cover. Scanning the skies, he was usually the first to see enemy planes in the distance. In the air he stayed cool and focused. He had the same ability he'd had in his hockey-playing days: while moving rapidly himself, he could keep track of everything that was moving around him.

What Jim kept to himself was that on the ground he often felt anxious. It didn't matter to him that the food was plain and monotonous, because he had little appetite. He ate lightly, just enough to keep up his energy and health.

Still, he liked the comradeship he found in 260. Jim

became good friends with several pilots in the squadron, including an Australian named Ron Cundy. Like Jim, Ron was a skilled pilot who still held the rank of sergeant. Ron had been in the Desert War since November 1941 and had never been hit. The two "colonials" discussed their dismay that in 260 Squadron, top and middle cover still flew in an old-fashioned RAF formation that they thought was impractical and unsafe.

In this formation, the planes flew in groups of six. There would be three section leaders flying ahead, and three pilots—the number two men—flying behind them, weaving from side to side. It was all these pilots could do to keep changing direction and still stay with their leaders. They had no time to look for enemy planes. And it was a formation that fell apart as soon as Messerschmitts attacked from above. Everyone ended up looking after their own tails. They were easy prey.

"You know," Jim said privately to Ron, "I think we're just there to distract the Me-109s from the bombers. Nobody even mentions tactics for fighting them." Ron had to agree with him. They both knew that the Finger Four formation was far safer and more effective for combat. Both of them hoped the day would come when they'd rise in the pecking order and be able to make some changes. Both men could take care of themselves, but they wanted to take care of the others as well.

* * *

With 260 Squadron, Jim would soon see some of the most intense air combat of the Desert War. The month of June 1942 was particularly stressful, as the desert squadrons threw everything they had at the advancing German army on the ground. For the first time, the Kittyhawks often carried bombs themselves. The ground crew brought the bombs out to the airfield in little carts and placed them in racks under the planes. A Kittyhawk could carry three 250-pound bombs— one under each wing and one under the fuselage, below the pilot. There was a switch in the cockpit to release the bombs.

Now each sortie was even more dangerous. As before, Jim and the other fighter pilots would escort bombers to the target, which now was the advancing German troops and vehicles on the ground. Then the Kittyhawks would drop their own bombs. And finally, they would dive in and strafe with their guns. On many of these missions, they also found themselves duelling with Messerschmitts that came swooping at them from above.

By the second week of June, Jim had damaged or destroyed four more enemy fighters. He finally felt that he had mastered the tricky Kittyhawk. Just as important to his survival, he had studied the tactics used by the attacking Messerschmitts. He had developed his own philosophy about fighting the air war: he would seize any chance to fire on an enemy plane, but he would never allow himself to be reckless. His motto became "To fly and do my job, and to live and fly again."

On June 17, Jim and other pilots from 260 were set upon by Messerschmitts while they were on a bomber-escort mission. As his own formation split apart under attack, Jim found himself wheeling and diving in a battle for his life. When an Me-109 closed in on him, he made a tighter turn than the enemy plane could manage (known as turning inside the enemy plane). The Messerschmitt, turning wider, overshot his Kitty-hawk. Now Jim was in position to get on *his* tail, and he quickly fired. The Messerschmitt flew away, losing altitude, with smoke pouring out of its engine.

When the brief, fierce battle was over, Jim saw that he was alone. He dove and flew low, constantly scanning the skies around him. It was dangerous to be alone over enemy territory, and he wanted to get back to base as fast as he could. But suddenly, about half a mile ahead, he spotted what he least wanted to see: more Messerschmitts.

Three were high above him, and one was near the ground, turning towards him—at least that is what it looked like. But in fact, the German pilot hadn't seen Jim. He had another target in his sights: a downed Canadian pilot in a desperate situation.

He was Wally Conrad, of 274 Hurricane Squadron. His plane had been fired on and damaged, but he had managed to make a forced landing. He crawled out of the cockpit, not seriously wounded, but with nowhere to hide on the desert floor. The pilot who had shot Wally down was coming after him to finish off both pilot and plane. He was so intent on his mission that he never saw Jim fire a burst that hit him broadside, sending his plane plummeting into the ground.

Jim sped off without watching the crash. There were three other Messerschmitts who might come after him, even though he couldn't see them any more. Perhaps they were already on their way back to base, unaware that one of their number had been lost. The German pilot had stayed around too long and had forgotten the cardinal rule: be aware at all times of what is around you. Jim flashed back briefly to the British pilot with haunted eyes who had warned him about the dangers of going down to see his handiwork. He was not about to make the mistake the German pilot had made.

As Jim flew back to base, he decided not to make a claim for the two Messerschmitts he had shot down. His new squadron leader was very strict about making claims, and Jim knew that no one from his squadron had witnessed his victories. He claimed only one "probable," for the first plane he had hit, which meant that its destruction was unconfirmed. However, in his own flight log, he put two black crosses as a reminder to himself of what he had done that day.

The desert pilots did not usually know who their opponents were. Only after the war did Jim learn that the second pilot he had shot down was a renowned German ace, Otto Schulz. He was known to the Luftwaffe as "Eins, zwei, drei" (one, two, three) Schulz for his sudden, deadly attacks. Schulz had destroyed fifty-one Allied planes, killing most of their pilots, including Imshi Mason, Jim's early squadron leader. He had almost added Wally Conrad to his score.

It wasn't until many years after the war that Jim met up with Wally Conrad. Conrad had finally learned from a military historian that it was Jim's plane that had saved his life, and he wanted to thank him. But Jim had to confess to Conrad that he hadn't actually noticed him; he'd only seen the downed Hurricane and the German plane diving on it.

Jim had to fly one more mission on June 17, in the early evening. He and his squadron mates duelled again with Messerschmitts, but all got back safely. All this happened on just one day in June. For June and most of July, Jim flew an average of more than two missions a day. The ground crews worked frantically to keep the planes in repair.

Not only were the pilots stretched to their limits during the day, but they were under bombardment at night. Jim took to sleeping in a slit trench with a piece of canvas rigged over it. It wasn't very comfortable, but it was better than scrambling out of his tent and jumping into the trench every time the German bombers came roaring out of the darkness.

Despite the intense Allied effort in the air and on the ground, first the line from Gazala to Bir Hacheim and then Tobruk itself fell to the Germans. As the German

Jim puts his cot in a slit trench for safety. He's on the left, and his squadron mate Bernie Bowerman is on the right.

army surged forward, Jim and his squadron were always near the front lines, covering the retreating Allied army. The distance to their targets was now so short that they called their flights "tram-raids." Every couple of days, they had to move back to a new landing ground. At these temporary bases, they had only the bare minimum of supplies. There was only enough water for drinking. Dirty and exhausted, they took off against the enemy, time and again. Five of the squadron's pilots were shot down within two weeks.

Even when he was not flying, Jim couldn't relax. He had to be ready to move back on very short notice. On the evening of June 28, he and Ron Cundy were sitting beside their planes, trying to rest. An army captain in a personnel carrier that was towing an anti-tank gun stopped by their planes and called out, "What are you fellows doing here?"

"Waiting for orders to move," Ron called back.

"Well, you'd better not wait too long," the captain replied. "Enemy tanks are less than two miles from here." Then his vehicle rumbled away in a cloud of dust.

But by the time the official order to move came from headquarters, it was already dark. Fortunately, there was a full moon to light their way. The squadron got away just in time. The ground crew's trucks pulled out of one side of the airfield as German trucks arrived on the other. Meanwhile, the pilots flew their Kittyhawks 20 miles east to a new landing ground. There, another ground crew awaited them. They had filled oil drums with sand soaked in gasoline and set it alight so that Jim and the other pilots could see where to land. They all made it safely.

As the sun came up the next morning, Jim could see the strain and exhaustion on every dirt-streaked face. How much longer can we go on like this? he thought.

Chapter 10

FIGHTER ACE

By the end of June 1942, the Egyptian cities of Cairo and Alexandria, where there were large British bases, were in a state of panic. German and Italian forces were less than 100 miles away. But between those cities and the enemy was the British army, which had dug in again at El Alamein. After a few days, it was clear that the Axis advance had been stopped.

When Jim had first arrived in Africa, it had been the Allied forces who were stretched to their limit. They had pushed westward as far as they could, and then for months they'd had to withdraw eastward. Now it was the Germans and Italians who had advanced as far as they could, and who had a long, slow supply line that was under attack. Without enough fuel and food, they could not continue.

Jim's squadron was based close to Alexandria, 40 miles behind the front line at El Alamein. The men were able to stay in one place for several months, and for the first time in weeks, they had fruit and vegetables. Fuel and replacements for damaged planes also arrived quickly.

Jim's mail from home finally caught up with him. In the summer heat, with daytime temperatures climbing past 100°F, he opened a parcel to find the hockey skates he had asked for months earlier. Another package contained one of his mother's Christmas cakes. It had been

A Christmas card that Jim sent to his mother from the desert.

sealed into a tin with solder, and it was still delicious. Jim and his squadron mates enjoyed it.

Jim's mother also sent news from home. His brother Bernie was in England with the 2nd Armoured Regiment, Lord Strathcona's Horse, training with tanks. His sister Dorothy had joined the WDs, the Women's Division of the RCAF, and had gone to Ottawa for training. Only his sister Jeanne and the two youngest boys, Leo and Wilfrid, remained at home. The boys were still in school, but they had joined the navy cadets. Snap was in good health and still missed him very much.

Although 260 Squadron now had more comfortable living conditions, there was no let-up in the Desert War. Jim continued to fly Kittyhawk bombing missions, now with a single 500-pound bomb strapped to the belly of his plane on each sortie. The Kittyhawks would escort the Boston bombers and then drop their bombs at the same time. Messerschmitts still attacked them on almost every run.

In the heat of combat, Jim rarely thought of the Luftwaffe pilots who were coming after him. Most often, he did not even see the other pilots as the planes swooped around each other. He concentrated on the machines, not the men. But on July 6, during Jim's forty-fifth operational sortie, it was different. Jim was escorting

Boston bombers when he saw Messerschmitts coming at them from above. At the same moment, his number two radioed that he had engine trouble and was heading back to base. Almost at once, Jim saw two Messerschmitts pursue the disabled plane. He turned to help out, and found that one of the Messerschmitts attacking his squadron mate was in his sights. He fired two bursts from astern, which connected with the Luftwaffe plane but didn't disable it. Closing with the plane, he fired again, but nothing happened—his guns had jammed!

Kittyhawk guns sometimes did this after turns and dives. Now Jim was in a battle for his life, with no guns. He banked and turned. The German pilot began to bank with him, but then pulled up and held his fire. Jim knew he was dealing with a veteran, who was waiting for the ideal deflection angle before finishing him off. As he completed his turn, Jim could see the Messerschmitt closing in behind him. He throttled back and lowered his flaps to make as tight a turn as he could. When he levelled out, he was facing the Messerschmitt nose to nose at about 300 yards. Jim held to his course. The German pilot veered at the last second, and the two planes barely missed each other. The shocked Luftwaffe pilot had been so busy avoiding a head-on collision that he never fired his guns. The two shaken pilots had both had enough. Each headed back to his home base.

As he flew home, Jim thought about what had just happened. This time, he had been very aware of another pilot using all the skills he had, just as Jim was. I'm saying a prayer in my cockpit, he thought, and the other pilot is probably saying a prayer to the same God. He's probably as good a type of fellow as I am. Jim shook his head at the ridiculousness of war. Later, he noted in his logbook, "Attacked by 109—very good pilot."

Jim had been raised never to hate anyone. He was very clear in his own mind that he did not hate his opponents—the individual German pilots. But he believed Germany's leaders had to be stopped. To keep Adolf Hitler and the Nazis from spreading their vile beliefs across the world, he would shoot down as many Luftwaffe planes as he could, without hesitating.

Jim had turned twenty-one during the heavy fighting in June. He was now a veteran of the desert air war. He often led sections, and sometimes he led the whole flight on combat missions, taking the responsibilities of a squadron leader, even though he was still a sergeant. Men of higher rank followed him willingly, because he was a leader they could trust. Ron Cundy was also leading officers. In the desert, experience and leadership ability counted for more than rank. However, one day Jim and Ron came back from a successful bomber escort to find that a very senior officer was paying a visit to the base. He was Air Vice-Marshal Arthur Coning-ham and he wasn't at all happy. "This kind of thing isn't done, old boy!" he spluttered at Jim. "Sergeant pilots just don't lead RAF squadrons."

Soon afterwards, Ron Cundy got his commission. Several months later, Jim finally received the commission he'd been denied back in Canada. In fact, he jumped several ranks, going directly from sergeant to flight lieutenant. (He skipped over the non-commissioned ranks of flight sergeant and warrant officer, as well as the commissioned ranks of pilot officer and flying officer.) Even though it didn't make much of a change in their responsibilities, he and Ron Cundy were both pleased with their promotions.

When there were lulls in the fighting, Jim and Ron used the time to train the newer pilots in Finger Four formation flying. The pilots learned how to make turns together, holding formation, when the leader called the turnabout over the radio or signalled it by dipping one wing. Jim had the pilots practise the turns alone and in pairs, "right on the deck" (just skimming over the desert floor). "You have to maintain the unit," he reminded the pilots over and over. "Stay together and stay alive."

Jim had always vowed that if he ever led men, he would respect them and explain things to them. Now he took the time to explain how to use the strengths of the Kittyhawk: its tight turns and its fast dives. And he explained that they should never climb when attacked by a Messerschmitt, because it could climb higher and faster than a Kittyhawk.

Jim had had many months to think about what made a top fighter pilot. He had come to realize that you couldn't judge a pilot by what you saw on the ground. A confident, outgoing man might be slow and hesitant in the air, while a quiet, reserved man might be quick and aggressive in combat. A pilot needed to have quick reflexes and keen eyesight, and he had to *use* that eyesight, staying aware of what was around him at all times. Although he was a very good teacher, Jim had to recognize his limits: he could try to teach the pilots to make the most of what they had, but he couldn't give them the gifts he had been born with. And he couldn't give them luck, which all pilots needed.

Allied forces had their backs to the wall at El Alamein. If they retreated any farther, the battle for control of the Suez Canal and the Mediterranean would be lost. Through the late summer and early autumn of 1942, the battle raged, and 260 Squadron was on the front lines.

On September 6, Jim and his fellow pilots faced their toughest test. They took off to intercept several Stuka bombers and their escort of Messerschmitt fighter planes. Jim was flying top cover, leading a section of four Kittyhawks. After only fifteen minutes of flying, he spotted the German formation, and minutes after that, two Me-109s peeled off from the other German fighter planes and attacked him from above. Jim turned his section to face the attackers, as they had practised. The Messerschmitts climbed quickly back to their own formation without firing. But that was just the beginning.

The Messerschmitts now tried attacking in pairs, from both ends at once. Swivelling his head constantly, Jim kept track of where they were and kept himself and his pilots out of range of their guns with one tight 360-degree turn after another. The pilots stayed with him and the formation held. At the same time, Jim was gradually moving his section back. The German pilots attacking them were being lured farther and farther away from their own lines. Then one of the Kittyhawks in Jim's section was hit and badly damaged, but the pilot was able to keep it in the air. Jim quickly fired on the attacking Messerschmitt and saw it turn for home, trailing black smoke from its engine.

The desperate manoeuvring went on for twenty minutes as pairs of Messerschmitts attacked again and again. Jim's section turned into them (turned to face them) dozens of times. They were exhausted, and Jim knew their formation could not hold much longer. Fortunately, the Messerschmitts, realizing how far they had strayed over Allied lines, gave up in frustration and flew away.

The shaken section landed their planes after an hour and twenty minutes in the air. With rubbery legs, they walked slowly to the operations tent. No one said a word. Then the pilot whose plane had been hit began to cry. None of the pilots who survived that battle ever forgot it. But they had survived it, under Jim's leadership.

A fighter ace was a pilot who had shot down five or more enemy planes. Since Jim had arrived in the desert he had shot down eight. Stories about his bravery appeared in Canadian newspapers, and his name was well known in North Africa. But the desert was a long way from the senior officers who decided who would receive medals.

Exhausted Jim (on the right) and squadron mate Jack Sheppard just after the September 6 battle. It was Sheppard's Kittyhawk that was hit by the Messerschmitt.

Furthermore, Jim was one of many Canadians serving in RAF squadrons in World War II; in fact, 60 percent of Canadian pilots served in RAF, not RCAF, squadrons. The Canadians sometimes felt they were overlooked by both services: the RAF because they weren't British, and the RCAF because they weren't serving under Canadian command. It wasn't until February 1943 that Jim learned he had been awarded the Distinguished Flying Medal (DFM). This was a decoration presented to non-commissioned officers, which Jim hadn't been for several months.

The citation read, in part, "He has displayed outstanding coolness and courage in the face of the opposition while his cheerful and imperturbable spirit has been an inspiration to the squadron." In the same month, Jim learned that he had also been awarded the Distinguished Flying Cross (DFC), which was for officers. He had been recommended for this decoration by a British army general. "In December 1942," that citation read, "Flight Lieutenant Edwards was commander of a formation engaged in patrol duties over our forward troops. During the flight 10 enemy aircraft were encountered and he destroyed one. . . . Two days later, he destroyed another hostile aircraft. . . . This officer has invariably displayed outstanding gallantry."

Jim's friend, Ron Cundy, was also awarded the DFM and the DFC, although he hadn't yet heard about it while he was with 260 Squadron. The Allies were also at war with Japan, and Japanese victories were bringing them closer and closer to Australia. Ron asked for a transfer back to his homeland. In December 1942, he left 260, headed for Australia. Jim was sorry to say goodbye to his friend. You couldn't be sure, in wartime, that you would ever see someone again.

Before leaving, Ron gave Jim the green polka-dot scarf that he wore around his neck. Scarves added dash to fighter pilots' uniforms, but they also had a practical purpose. A scarf kept a pilot's neck from getting chafed by his collars as he constantly turned his head to check for enemy planes.

After the battle of El Alamein, the Axis forces were in retreat. But it took months of hard fighting before they were driven back through Egypt and Libya into Tunisia. The United States had now entered the war, and in November 1942, American troops landed in North Africa. German and Italian troops were trapped between the American and British armies, and they finally surrendered in May 1943.

Jim's squadron was in the campaign right to the end. By then, Jim had flown almost 200 operational sorties and shot down more than fifteen planes, damaging many more in the air. He had also destroyed twelve aircraft on the ground. But the war had been costly for the squadron. Thirty-three pilots had been killed, ten of them Canadians, and twelve more had been seriously wounded.

Today the role of Canadian servicemen in the war in North Africa is not as well remembered as their actions in Europe. But the North African campaign marked the first time in World War II that the Germans were defeated on the ground. German and Italian forces were pushed out of North Africa, with 275,000 troops taken prisoner, and they never returned there during the war.

It was the end of one phase of the war, but Jim still had many combat missions ahead of him.

Chapter 11

A CRASH IN ITALY

The young pilots gazed upward. Some of their faces wore frowns of concentration, and some had mouths open in amazement. Their instructor, Jim Edwards, was demonstrating a quarter attack—from slightly above and to the side—at a target drogue being towed by another plane. He fired nine 20-mm cannon shells at the drogue from his Spitfire. He shredded the target and, with his final shot, cut the tow rope. Even more awe-inspiring to the students who watched him, he did this while flying his plane upside down. Jim was trying to convince them, in the most dramatic way he knew, that accurate firing was possible. He could do it, and he would do his best to teach them to do it, too.

After the North African campaign ended, Jim had been taken out of combat and made an instructor at the Middle East Central Gunnery School in El Ballah,

Egypt. He wasn't too happy about that, but he understood it. He had shot down nineteen enemy planes in
the desert, and damaged many more. The air force
thought he should pass on his skills. The best part of the
gunnery school, for Jim, was that he finally got to fly
Spitfires. A senior officer promised him that if he taught
for six months, he would be sent back to active service.

The officer kept his word, and in December 1943,
Jim joined 417 Squadron, based near Termoli, Italy, on
the Adriatic Sea. This was the first time that he had
served with a Canadian squadron. And at long last, he
was flying Spitfires in combat. They were easy to
manoeuvre and very fast. To really appreciate this
plane, Jim thought, you have to have flown a Kittyhawk
in combat first.

While Jim was at the gunnery school, the war around
the Mediterranean Sea had moved into a new phase.
With the southern shore of the Mediterranean
secured, the Allies had turned their attention to Italy,
which was Germany's ally. British, Commonwealth
and American troops had invaded the island of Sicily in
July 1943 and captured it by August. Italy announced
its surrender on September 8, but German forces in
Italy continued to fight fiercely. Allied troops would
now have to fight their way up the long "boot" of Italy.
In September they invaded Salerno and Taranto, and

Flight Lieutenant Jim Edwards,
wearing Ron Cundy's polka-dot scarf.
(Ron is wearing it himself in the picture on page 67.)

by October they held Naples, on the Mediterranean coast. By the time Jim arrived in Italy, the Germans had been pushed back to a line that ran through Cassino. In North Africa, he had often thought that he must have a guardian angel watching over him, and in Italy he needed one more than ever.

After just ten sorties with 417, Jim was transferred to 92 Squadron of the RAF, as a flight commander. The squadron soon moved from the Adriatic coast to the Mediterranean coast, to provide air support for the Allied invasion of Anzio, a port 30 miles south of Rome.

In the middle of February, Jim was leading his flight of twelve planes into an attack on a formation of Focke-Wolf 190s and Messerschmitt 109s. However, one of the pilots did not follow Jim's commands. Instead of staying in formation with the others, he flew straight into the German formation. Jim's planned attack broke apart in confusion, and soon he was in a battle for his life.

He wheeled and turned to fire on Messerschmitts that were closing in on his pilots, shooting down several. Then he dove after one Focke-Wolf that was trying to get away and finally hit it with a burst of machine-gun fire just a few hundred feet above the ground. But almost at the same moment, his Spitfire shook with a violent explosion.

Jim's plane began to buck and shudder. All through the frenzied air battle, his wingman had managed to stay with him. Over the radio, Jim asked the wingman to fly up beside him and tell him what was wrong. The answer was a shock: "I can see right through your plane!"

A shell fired from the ground had blown a hole 12 inches in diameter right through his Spit, just behind the cockpit. Miraculously it had not exploded, nor had it damaged anything vital. Jim was able to nurse his wounded airplane back to his base.

By now, Jim had learned in a letter from home that Bernie was also in Italy. He was fighting the Germans on the ground, driving a tank in the 2nd Armoured regiment. But the two brothers never managed to meet up.

In March, Jim was promoted to squadron leader and given command of 274 Squadron of the RAF. This was a famous squadron that had served bravely in North Africa. Jim was excited to be in command of veterans of that war, many of them high-scoring aces. However, after just a few missions with his new squadron, he had a terrible accident.

Twelve planes from 274 Squadron, with Jim in the lead, took off from Termoli for a strafing mission near Rome, which was still in German hands. Jim was climbing over the Apennines, the mountain range that runs down the middle of Italy, when his plane developed a glycol leak. Glycol was the fluid that kept the engine cool. Without it, the engine of Jim's Spitfire quickly overheated. The cockpit filled with choking white smoke.

Jim made a quick decision to bail out, and unhooked his safety harness. He struggled to open the canopy on his plane. But as soon as he had a clear view, he realized it was too late to bail. He was so close to the rugged mountain peaks that his chute wouldn't have time to open. There was nothing to do but make a forced landing. But where?

Then he saw it—a small clearing right on top of the mountain. It would have to do, and he headed for it. He was just about to touch down, thinking he'd made it through another tight spot, when the engine blew up. Jim didn't even hear the explosion. It just seemed to him that, faster than thought, everything went black.

Flying overhead, his stunned squadron mates circled the wreckage, watching flames consume the Spitfire. They saw no movement on the ground. They returned to their base, reporting that their popular squadron leader had been lost.

Jim awoke to see a beautiful woman in a white veil bending over him. He struggled to speak. A raspy voice he hardly recognized croaked, "Am I in heaven?" The woman smiled and said, "Don't worry, you're with friends." Her lips kept moving, but he couldn't hear her and he was gone again.

The next time Jim woke up, his head felt much clearer. The woman was with him again, and this time he recognized her as a military nurse. The veil was part of her uniform. Over the next couple of days, he pieced together the story of how he had been rescued. He had been incredibly lucky. Normally, he would have been strapped in while landing, but he had undone his harness when he prepared to bail out. As the plane crashed, he was thrown clear of the flames. But he was unconscious, badly injured and alone.

By chance, though, someone had seen him come down: the rugged men of a Gurkha gun battery high in the mountains. (Gurkhas were soldiers from Nepal who had a long history of fighting for Britain.) They made their way over to Jim and took him down the mountain on a stretcher to a field hospital set up in an old farmhouse. There a doctor put thirteen stitches in the back of Jim's head and eleven over his right eye. He had bruises all over his body and a black eye that wouldn't fade for months.

Jim never did find out how long he'd been in the hospital. However, on the first day that he was able to sit up and eat, he decided that he wanted to leave. He wasn't in pain, he was the squadron leader, his men needed him, and he had to get back to them at once. He asked for his clothes and struggled into them. Before anyone could stop him, Jim walked to the main road passing the hospital and hitched a ride.

When Jim strode onto the base, unannounced, the pilots were in the middle of a briefing for their next mission. Their jaws dropped and they stared as if they were looking at a ghost. Jim had a huge white gauze bandage wrapped around and around his head, and down over his right eye. The part of his face that showed was almost as pale as the bandage. Everyone had believed he was dead. In fact, their new squadron leader was scheduled to arrive the next day. But after a moment of shocked silence, they surged towards him, congratulating him and ushering him to a chair.

As it turned out, Jim would be in Italy for only a few more days, and he never led 274 Squadron over Italy again. The whole squadron was ordered back to England. Jim had now flown 278 sorties in the war, and had shot down more than twenty enemy planes. It was April 1944, and he was still only twenty-two years old. He was about to play a role in the largest military landing in history.

Chapter 12

D-DAY AND AFTER

After a ten-day leave, Jim's squadron, 274, and two other squadrons, 80 and 249, formed a new Spitfire wing at RAF station Hornchurch, on the east side of London. At Hornchurch, Jim was back in a world he had almost forgotten existed. He slept in a bed with sheets and blankets. As Squadron Leader Edwards, he ate good food served in the comfort of the officers' mess. His laundry was gathered up and came back clean and pressed. He wore a blue uniform with shiny brass buttons and an officer's hat. But like most fighter pilots, he left the top button of his tunic undone, and around his neck he wore the polka-dot scarf Ron Cundy had given him

Jim was still wearing a bandage on his head, but it was now small enough that he could fit his flying helmet over it. The skin around his right eye and down one side of his face was still bruised in shades of purple, green and yellow. But the doctors who examined him in England reassured him that his sight had not been damaged.

It was now the spring of 1944. Although the war in Europe still had many months to go, it was becoming clear that the Allies would eventually win it. German cities were under heavy attack by Allied bombing raids. On the ground, the German forces were being pushed, slowly but relentlessly, out of Italy. In the east, the Russian army had repelled the Germans and was now fighting them in Poland. The Russians were getting closer and closer to Berlin.

There had been rumours among Allied troops for months that their forces would soon cross the Channel from England and attack the Germans in France. The Germans expected the invasion, too, but they had no idea where along the coast of France it would occur. That was a closely guarded secret, known only to a handful of Allied generals.

Meanwhile, Jim led 274 Squadron on sweeps over German-occupied France and escorted bombers as they hit bridges and enemy aerodromes. He was flying a beautiful new plane, the latest Spitfire model. But the RAF pilots saw no enemy aircraft. It was as if the Luftwaffe had disappeared.

June 5, 1944, was Jim's twenty-third birthday, and he felt very lucky to have reached it. So many of the men he had flown with in Africa and Italy had not. That

evening, Jim and the other pilots were called to a briefing. They were told that the next morning would be
D-Day: the largest amphibious (from water to land)
force in history was going to cross the English Channel
and land on the beaches of Normandy, France. The
long-awaited invasion, which the Allies hoped would
push the Germans back within their own borders and
defeat them, was finally under way. Jim's squadron was
going to provide air cover.

A senior RAF officer at the briefing noticed Jim's
bandage and multi-coloured face and asked if he was fit
for the challenge ahead. "Yes, sir, I'm absolutely fine,
sir," Jim replied. "Jolly good show!" said the officer.

In the early morning hours of June 6, Jim was awed by
his overhead view of the invasion. The Channel was
filled, as far as the eye could see, with ships and troop
carriers heading from England to Normandy. The
Channel waters were grey and choppy, with the wind
kicking up whitecaps on three-foot waves. He could see
troops struggling ashore under fire from the German
gun batteries. At the same time, Allied destroyers off-
shore shelled ahead of the troops as they landed to give
them some protection.

Aircraft swarmed around Jim in the sky. Allied planes
had been painted with black-and-white stripes for the
invasion, so they could easily be distinguished from

On D-Day, a convoy of ships carries Canadians towards Juno Beach on the Normandy coast. Barrage balloons float in the sky as protection from air attack.

enemy planes. But during the three flights Jim made on June 6, and again on June 7, he saw no enemy planes. Still, there was danger from the German guns below.

Jim's 274 Squadron had been assigned to escorting Halifaxes, Dakotas and other twin-engine and four-engine planes. The planes towed enormous wooden Horsa gliders at the end of heavy hemp ropes. Each glider could carry thirty soldiers. The flight formation stretched from one shore to the other across the English Channel.

All the gliders were supposed to land in the same area, behind the German coastal defences. When they were over their landing spots, the tow planes released the ropes and the gliders swooped down to land. Jim sometimes saw planes heading towards the wrong field, but he had no radio communication with them, so he couldn't warn them. Far worse, heavy flak from the ground brought down many of the tow planes. Then the helpless gliders would crash among the enemy guns. It was a horrible, heartbreaking sight. Jim had seen many planes shot down, piloted by friends and foes. But these were not airmen who could try to defend themselves; they were soldiers who never even had a chance to fight.

Still, as costly as they were in lives lost, the glider landings were successful, as was the overall invasion. Allied troops were now in France, and pushing inland.

For the rest of June and into July, Jim led fighter sweeps, bomber escorts and strafing sorties across the Channel to France. His squadron remained based in England, however, to his frustration. Although they landed a few times on the beachhead to refuel, there was no room for them at the small landing fields in France.

Jim's 274 Squadron mates sometimes saw German fighter planes off in the distance, but never had the chance to engage them. However, they did have close encounters with some advanced German technology. On June 28, while providing high cover to a formation of Lancaster bombers over northeast France, Jim spotted a small, incredibly fast plane, whizzing and zipping around the sky. It looked to him like an angry bumblebee trapped in a small room. But the pilot made no attempt to attack Jim's formation, so he decided the plane must be on a test flight. Later he learned that it was a Messerschmitt Komet, a rocket-propelled fighter plane.

The other encounter happened the same day, just as Jim and his fellow pilots, flying in tight formation, crossed the south coast of England on their way home. Jim spotted a small object approaching them at the same altitude and at a 60-degree angle. He eased the control stick forward and the rest of the formation instantly followed him down. The object—an unmanned German V-1 rocket—skimmed over the top of the formation, just missing it.

Thousands of V-1 rockets rained down on England, and especially on London, through the summer of 1944. The British called them buzz bombs because of the sound their engines made. It was nerve-wracking listening to the rockets fly overhead; at the moment the engine noise cut out, Londoners knew the bomb was about to plummet down and explode.

In early August, Jim's squadron was re-equipped with Tempest fighter planes, which were faster than Spitfires. The pilots' new assignment was to try to intercept V-1s. However, just a few weeks after the squadron got its Tempests, the RCAF ordered Jim back to Canada for some rest. He had flown 350 operational sorties in the war, more than he was supposed to without a break. Jim believed that the RCAF had lost track of him for a time, as he moved from North Africa to Italy and to England, allowing him to continue flying.

Jim was disappointed that he was being taken out of combat. He had hoped to be promoted to wing commander, with several squadrons under his command, before the war ended. That was the highest rank you could hold and still fly regular combat missions. The one bright spot was that before boarding a ship for Canada, he was awarded a Bar to his Distinguished Flying Cross. This was like winning a second DFC.

The Canadian government asked Jim, as a decorated fighter ace, to go on a tour. He was to make speeches and sell war bonds, which were sold to the Canadian public to help finance the war. Fortunately, the tour was in his home province of Saskatchewan. He had a wonderful reunion with his parents and his two younger brothers. Bernie was still fighting somewhere in Italy, and his sister Jeanne had followed her older sister in joining the war effort. She was now in the Canadian Women's Army Corps and stationed in Regina. Jim was sad to find out, however, that Snap had passed away a short while before he returned home.

For the next three weeks, Jim was expected to make a speech every weekday, usually in the afternoon or evening. By now it was fall, so he used the mornings to go duck hunting or pheasant hunting. He thought fondly of the old companion who used to romp along beside him so eagerly.

When Jim's bond tour was finished, the air force sent him to headquarters in Winnipeg, where he had few duties. However, the air force had a hockey team there, called the Blue Bombers, and Jim began to play with them. Most of the team members had been professional hockey players before the war. Jim enjoyed getting back to his favourite game, but he felt hard pressed to keep up with them.

Next he was sent to the Service Flying Training School in Calgary to get some experience flying twin-engine planes. Jim had little interest in this, but he dutifully flew Ansons and Cranes, the training planes, and wondered when the air force would let him get back to the war. Again, he got to play some hockey, for the Stampeders, another air force team. He was still playing with pros, but now he was back in shape and able to score. Although he was the smallest man on his team, players on other teams rarely touched him. He was usually fast enough to elude them, and when that wasn't the case, the bigger men on his own team looked out for him. They let it be known that there would be retaliation if Jim was injured.

But Jim had not been forgotten overseas. The air force was looking for wing commanders for operations in Europe. Jim's leadership qualities were just what the RCAF needed. He was called back to take command of 127 Wing, which was made up of four Canadian squadrons: 443, 421, 416 and 403. All of them had distinguished war records, especially 403, which had been the first RCAF squadron formed overseas. It had 115 air victories.

Taking command of his own wing had been Jim's dream, and now it had come true.

When Jim returned to Europe to take command in the spring of 1945, American and Commonwealth forces were already pushing into Germany from the west. Meanwhile, their Russian allies had entered Germany from the east. But the Germans were still fighting back desperately. Luftwaffe pilots were still taking to the air, although their numbers had dwindled and they had few airfields left that they could use.

Jim's squadrons strafed and bombed railway lines and marshalling yards, and destroyed as much German military equipment on the ground as they could. Although they seldom had opposition in the air, Allied

Wing Commander James F. Edwards,
with his personal Spitfire. Note the letters JFE.

planes were still being shot down and pilots being killed by flak from the ground. In early April, Jim's Spitfire was hit by a flak shell while he was attacking German gunboats in the Kiel Canal—only the second time in the war he had been hit. Again, he was very lucky. The shell went straight through the port (left) wing, taking out the cannon. He was still able to fly it back to base.

At the end of April, Jim was flying a patrol near Hamburg, Germany, when he saw a Messerschmitt 262. This was a new German plane, and the first jet Jim had ever seen in the air. He was amazed that the Germans were still able to roll out advanced new designs so late in the war. He pursued the fighter jet and fired at it, but it zipped away into the clouds. It crossed his mind that he would like to fly a plane like that one day.

On May 3, 1945, Jim flew his 373rd, and last, combat mission of the war. He was leading 443 Squadron over Kiel, Germany, when they spotted a lone enemy aircraft. He and other members of his squadron fired at it until it went down. It was a Junkers 88—just like the very first German aircraft he had ever seen, bombing his first base in North Africa. Less than a week later, Germany surrendered and the war in Europe was over.

Chapter 13

STARTING OVER

It is not easy to come home from a war. From the age of nineteen, Jim's life had often been stressful and dangerous, but it had also been organized and simple: get up, seek out the enemy, fight and come back to base. He had been a fighter pilot, a good one, and he had also developed into a leader of men. But he had not allowed himself to think beyond the end of the war. Now peace had come, and he was still only twenty-four years old. He had to figure out where he fit in.

Unlike soldiers, who usually came home in regiments, air force pilots came home by ones and twos. There were no brass bands and cheers to greet them. Once again, though, Jim was whisked off on a bond tour. He didn't see a large group of air force combat veterans until December 1945, when he reached

Yorkton, Saskatchewan. The base where he had taken his Service Flying Training and received his wings had been turned into a centre to process hundreds of returning air force men. They were known as "repats" (from the word "repatriated," meaning returned to your home country).

Here Jim caught up with old friends he hadn't seen during the war years. The survivors took stock of who had made it through the war and who had not. (Canada had provided 94,000 men for the RCAF and RAF, and more than 17,000 of these had been killed.) Now that he was not in combat every day, Jim could afford to let himself think a little more about the friends he had lost.

As well as old friends, a nickname found Jim again at Yorkton. The name dated back to a heated table tennis game that took place at Yorkton when he was still in training in 1940. Jim was winning game after game, and his opponent took offence. He was a much bigger man, and he tried to start a fist fight with Jim. A friend of Jim's, Ken Goldie, was just about to step in when he saw that Jim could handle the larger man perfectly well. The fight ended quickly, with no real damage done. Ken said to him, "Well, Jim, I'd say you're stocky, blocky and cocky." After that, his friends at Yorkton always called him Stocky.

The nickname got lost in the war years, but now it started up again, and this time it stuck. Soon everyone on a first-name basis with Jim called him Stocky—it just seemed to suit his no-nonsense personality. As it turned out, Stocky was going to need all his determination and strength of character over the next few years.

Stocky had decided that he wanted to remain in the air force, which had been his whole world for the past five years. But there were thousands of Canadian fighter pilots returning home from the war now. The RCAF was not sure what to do with them. The Canadian government had not yet decided how large the peacetime air force should be, or what its role would be in the new post-war world.

Senior officers who had spent all or most of the war in Canada would now decide Stocky's future. It often seemed to Stocky that these officers were more interested in protecting their own jobs than they were in finding a meaningful role for a former fighter ace. Some of them had decided before they even met him that young pilots with chests full of medals must be conceited and irresponsible. Stocky found that defending himself and hanging on to his officer's rank in peacetime was far more challenging than aerial combat.

The first setback came when a fire destroyed the mess at Yorkton on Christmas Eve. The repats' processing centre moved to Centralia, Ontario, about 50 miles from Sarnia. Stocky was put in charge, with the rank of acting wing commander.

In February, at a Valentine's dance, Stocky met an air force nurse named Alice Antonio, known to her friends as "Toni." They dated several times, but then Toni was transferred to Trenton, Ontario. It seemed that nothing more would come of this relationship.

Soon after, Stocky became commanding officer of the Centralia base. At the same time, however, he lost his wing commander rank and was demoted to squadron leader. Stocky wasn't happy about that, but he knew that many men who had advanced quickly in combat were now having their ranks reduced as the peacetime air force became smaller. Later, his rank was bumped down again, to flight lieutenant on a short-service commission. This meant that he would be re-evaluated in five years. If he could "prove himself," he would then be considered for a permanent commission. This was the last straw for a proud young man who had risked his life for his country. Didn't that count as proving himself?

Stocky went to see his Member of Parliament in Ottawa and explained to him why he deserved a permanent commission. The MP knew that Stocky was a popular man in his riding of Battleford. "I'll see what I can do," he said. "Well, I'm not leaving this office until this is straightened out," Stocky replied. The MP got on the phone to a high-ranking officer—an air vice marshal—who knew Stocky and respected his achievements. After the air vice marshal got involved, Stocky received his permanent commission.

In June 1946, Stocky married a nurse named Norma Alice Hatcher. It was one of the few bright spots in his life, as bad luck continued to dog him. The newlyweds were planning to move to Toronto so that Stocky could take an air force administration course for officers. However, just before the move, he broke his leg in two places, sliding into third base in an air force baseball game. For a time, he had to wear a full leg cast. Even after he got the cast off, it was a struggle to get around. But he managed to complete the course with good marks.

When Stocky had finished the course, he learned to his shock and disgust that he was to be posted to the RCAF station at Trenton, to tow drogues at a gunnery school. Again, he protested strongly. This time, a decision made by the Canadian government came to his rescue. The RCAF was to buy 100 Vampire jets, and they would need fighter pilots to fly them and instruct other pilots. They decided that auxiliary squadrons would get Canada's first jets. The auxiliaries were reserve squadrons that could be called up in time of need. The pilots trained regularly, but otherwise went about their civilian lives.

Stocky's skills were once more in demand. He became one of Canada's first jet pilots in 1947, fulfilling an ambition he had had since he first saw a German jet during the war. Soon he was the commanding officer of a base in St. Hubert, Quebec (near Montreal). There he was in charge of regular air force staff, and also trained pilots in auxiliary Squadrons 438 and 401 on Vampire jets.

His personal life was happy, too. The Edwardses had a daughter, Dorothy, born while they were in Toronto. Another daughter, Jeanne, was born in Montreal. But when Jeanne was four months old, Stocky's wife caught polio—a dreaded disease in the days before the vaccine—and died.

Nothing that happened to Stocky during the war could compare to the grief and shock he felt now. His wife's sister came to help him care for his two young children, but he felt that it was impossible for him to remain in St. Hubert. He requested a posting and was soon on his way to British Columbia. He took his young children and his sister-in-law with him. In BC, he was in charge of a search-and-rescue operation at RCAF Station Sea Island. Stocky felt uncomfortable commanding this base with no rescue experience, however, and later switched to working in a Vancouver recruiting depot.

And now Stocky and Toni Antonio's paths crossed again. After her discharge from the air force, Toni had become a nurse in Vancouver. In 1949, when she heard that Stocky's wife had died, she had written to express her sympathy. After he arrived in Vancouver, Stocky wrote to her, inviting her to dinner. She accepted his invitation and soon they were dating again. They were married at the Holy Rosary Cathedral in Vancouver on February 3, 1951.

Stocky and Toni's wedding,
February 3, 1951.

Toni became a loving mother to Stocky's two children. As the wife of a military man, she had to be
resourceful at creating a home wherever they were
posted. In the first few years of their marriage, that
included St. Hubert (a second time for Stocky) and

North Bay, where Stocky formed and led 430 Squadron, a regular RCAF squadron that flew F-86 Sabre jets.

In 1952, Stocky finally regained his wartime rank of wing commander, and an important new assignment.

In the years after World War II, the Soviet Union and the United States, which had been allies during the war, became the world's greatest military powers. With very different economic and political systems, they competed for influence over other countries. These years of intense rivalry, which lasted from the end of World War II until the break-up of the Soviet Union in the early 1990s, were known as the Cold War.

The nations of Western Europe feared that the Communist Soviet Union, which controlled much of Eastern Europe after the war, would try to take them over, too. In 1949, the United States, Canada and ten nations in Europe signed an agreement to create the North Atlantic Treaty Organization (NATO). The nations pledged to co-operate to defend themselves. As part of its obligations to NATO, Canada was to provide fighter squadrons that would be based in Europe.

Stocky commanded Number 2 Fighter Wing, which was made up of three RCAF squadrons: 430, 416 and 421. After a ceremony at Uplands air force base in Ottawa, Stocky led the three squadrons of F-86 Sabres

*Stocky in the cockpit of his F-86 Sabre,
departing for Grostenquin, France.*

on a flight to Grostenquin, France, with refuelling
stops at Goose Bay, Labrador; Bluie West in Green-
land; Keflavik, Iceland; and Prestwick, Scotland.

When Stocky arrived, he found the Grostenquin
base still under construction. The base was a sea of

mud, with unfinished buildings, no electricity and no fuel for the aircraft. Gradually conditions improved, until he could bring Toni and the children—now including baby Debi—to live with him. Home was a trailer parked near the end of a runway. At first, the children woke up in alarm every time a plane took off, but they soon learned to sleep through it.

The Edwards family made many more moves over the years. Some of their happiest times were in Colorado Springs, Colorado, where Stocky had two important postings to NORAD, the North American

Stocky and his family in Colorado Springs, Colorado, in the 1960s. From left: Debi, Stocky, Dorothy, Toni, Jeanne and Jim.

Air Defense Command. (Later the A-word in the name was changed to "Aerospace.") This is a joint Canadian–American operation that was founded in 1958 to protect airspace over North America. In Colorado Springs, among other assignments, Stocky worked on a computer system called SAGE (Semi Automatic Ground Environment), which could track enemy aircraft. He devised various types of air attacks and responses that could be used for simulations. By now, the Edwards family had grown to four children, with the birth of James ("Jim") in 1955.

Stocky retired from the air force in 1972 and settled with his family in Comox, British Columbia.

Chapter 14

STOCKY TODAY

Stocky Edwards is in his eighties now, still trim and active. He and Toni live in the comfortable Comox home they had built for them in 1972, with a beautiful view of Comox Bay. Stocky, his eyesight still keen, takes pleasure in watching eagles soaring and swooping over the bay like fighter planes, and seeing seals splashing and diving in the water below. Stocky and Toni can go for long walks and play golf almost year round in the mild Vancouver Island climate. Some sixty years after they first met at a Valentine's dance, they still enjoy dancing together.

Comox is home to many air force people, and Stocky and Toni are part of that circle. They are members of 888 Wing, which is like the Royal Canadian Legion for air force veterans and their spouses. The organization has many social events and also sponsors 386

Squadron of the Royal Canadian Air Cadets. Stocky is often asked to pin wings on graduating air force cadets at the Regional Gliding School, which runs every summer at the 19 Wing Canadian Forces Base in Comox. Stocky is also a keen supporter of the Comox Air Force Museum, which is currently involved in restoring a Spitfire fighter plane. Stocky is a sought-after speaker at mess dinners, fighter pilot reunions and other events across Canada.

Stocky and Toni's son, Jim, a teacher, and daughter Debi (who in her singing career goes by the name of Angel) also live in British Columbia, so they are able to see them often. Sadly, their daughter Jeanne, a talented artist, died of cancer in January 1998.

Stocky in the cockpit of a Kittyhawk, summer 2002.

Their daughter Dorothy lives on her farm near Pembroke, Ontario for most of the year. However, in the spring and summer, she goes to the High Arctic as a chef for scientific expeditions. Her experiences are sometimes similar to the ones her father had long ago, if you replace sand with snow. In the spring of 2005, she had a close call when she and a group of scientists were out on the ice. A late storm swept all but one of their tents away. When the pegs of the last tent began to pop out, they had to sit on its edges for hours, to keep their final shelter from blowing away as well. Stocky and Toni were very relieved when the whole team was rescued.

Stocky's brother Bernie survived the war and lived in Battleford for the rest of his life. He died in 1986, and his sister Dorothy died in 2004. Stocky's youngest sister and two younger brothers are still alive, and he sees them often. By 2005, Stocky and Toni had also been blessed with eight grandchildren and five great-grandchildren.

Although many of the men Stocky flew with did not survive the war, both Bill Barker (who never served in the same squadron with Jim after the voyage to England) and Ron Cundy did. Stocky is still in touch with both of them. In 2001, Ron Cundy wrote a book about the Desert War called *A Gremlin on My Shoulder*, in which Jim and their friendship play an important role.

* * *

THE DESERT HAWK

Stocky had always thought that he would like to try his hand at painting, but during his air force career he had never found the time. One day in 1972, he stopped into an art-supply store in Comox. He spent some time looking over the wonderful range of art materials, and finally settled on the rich array of oil paints. He asked the woman behind the counter, "How would I go about doing an oil painting?" The woman gave him some basic instruction about preparing his canvas and applying the paint. Then he filled up a shopping bag with supplies and returned home happily. He had always been able to master anything he set his mind to, by breaking things down into logical steps and developing his skills with patience and persistence. He was confident he could do the same with painting.

For his first painting, he chose a subject he remembered vividly from his prairie boyhood: geese flying over Saskatchewan grasslands. He planned the whole picture in his head until he could see clearly where everything should go. Then he drew it on paper and traced it onto his canvas before starting the painting. It was the beginning of an absorbing new interest. Stocky has now done more than a hundred paintings, of geese, ducks, eagles and also warplanes, including the Kittyhawk on the cover of this book.

As he focused on the beauty and grace of birds for his paintings, he lost all desire to hunt them. Today Stocky concentrates on fly fishing in nearby waters for salmon and trout, which Toni then cooks for dinner. He patiently ties his own flies, which are beautiful, iridescent works of art.

In 1983, Stocky published a memoir, *Kittyhawk Pilot*, which he co-wrote with Michel Lavigne. He followed this in 2002 with a large-scale illustrated book, also with Lavigne, called *Kittyhawks over the Sands.* A third book, *Hurricanes over the Sands,* came out in 2003, and they are planning a second volume about the Hurricanes.

In March 2004, Stocky got a phone call from Rideau Hall, the Ottawa residence of the Governor General, asking him if he would accept the Order of Canada. This is the highest civilian honour that a Canadian can receive. It recognizes a lifetime of outstanding service to the nation. Stocky, of course, said yes.

Each year, there are several Order of Canada investiture ceremonies—events where people receive the award from the Governor General. It was agreed that Stocky would come to Ottawa for the ceremony in December. The next few months were an exciting time for the Edwardses. Stocky received letters of congratulation from the prime minister, the premier of British Columbia and many other well-wishers.

On the afternoon of December 10, 2004, Governor General Adrienne Clarkson pinned the Order of Canada on Stocky's blue blazer. Toni, grandson Tracey and granddaughter Jessie looked on proudly. Also receiving the Order that day in the elegant blue ballroom at Rideau Hall were scientists, artists, writers and other outstanding Canadians.

In the evening, the Order of Canada recipients were honoured with a reception and a formal dinner at Rideau Hall. Stocky had changed into his mess kit— his dress uniform—and Toni was now wearing an evening gown. Before dinner, in the festive-striped Tent Room, the Governor General and her husband, John Ralston Saul, chatted to Stocky and the other guests. He was charmed by their warmth. Later in the evening, relaxed after an excellent dinner, Stocky was asked by the Governor General's husband if he would speak to the gathering for about ten minutes. Stocky had been given no warning, so that he wouldn't be nervous during dinner. But he quickly marshalled his thoughts. What would he like to say on this important occasion?

After he was introduced and had thanked his hosts, Stocky looked around the room at the other recipients of the Order, and paused. "All the people in this room tonight are here because they had something to offer Canada," he began. "They used their talents to strengthen our country. In our national anthem, it says 'We stand on guard for thee.' What do we mean when we say that? Are we prepared to stand up for Canada? In my generation, the answer was simple. We were ready to fight for our country to save it from its enemies. Today, we have to ask ourselves what standing up for Canada means. I think it means that we have to be proud of being Canadian. Whatever else we are, no matter what our religion or our race, we have to think of ourselves as Canadians, and tell the world who we are and the values we stand for."

Stocky's speech was met with enthusiastic applause. He had spoken from his heart.

Stocky and Toni, December 2004.
Stocky has just received the Order of Canada.

A NOTE ON NAMES

James Francis Edwards has been known by several names in his lifetime. His family and friends called him Jimmy when he was a little boy, and Jim as he grew up. During World War II, many servicepeople, both men and women, acquired a nickname based on their last names. So, in the air force, Jim Edwards became "Eddie." After the war, he became widely known as Stocky. To avoid confusion in *The Desert Hawk*, I used only the names Jim and Stocky.

A NOTE ON ACES

In World War II, just as in World War I, the working definition of an ace was a pilot who had achieved at least five confirmed victories in air-to-air combat (as opposed to destroying planes on the ground). James Edwards was a high-ranking Canadian ace of World War II. His official record was seventeen destroyed (confirmed by a witness or by downed aircraft on the ground), ten probables (likely but not confirmed) and eight destroyed on the ground. However, his achievement is even more remarkable, for several reasons.

First, Jim achieved many of his victories while flying a Kittyhawk, a plane that was technically inferior to the German Messerschmitts he fought. (RAF and Commonwealth aces in Europe achieved most of their victories flying in Spitfires, which were much faster and more manoeuvrable than Kittyhawks.)

Second, it was extremely difficult, in the heat of combat, for any fighter pilot to tally victories. After the war, when Allied and German claims could be compared, it was clear that both sides had claimed more victories than they had actually achieved. However, Jim had most of his victories with 260 Squadron, whose squadron leader was unusually strict about his pilots' claims. Additionally, Jim was focused only on doing his job, not on becoming an ace. Sometimes he did not bother to put in a claim. Sometimes he shared a claim with another pilot, feeling that it would be good for the other man's confidence.

Jim did keep track privately of the planes he believed he had destroyed or damaged. After the war, when his records were compared to German records, it became clear that his real, although unofficial, score was higher: twenty-two destroyed, as well as two shared destroyed and six probables. In addition, he destroyed twelve enemy aircraft on the ground and damaged fifteen more. According to Michel Lavigne, co-author of *Kittyhawks over the Sands*, James Edwards was a rare fighter ace of World War II who actually destroyed *more* enemy aircraft than he claimed.

GLOSSARY

Allies: Led by Britain (and the Commonwealth countries), the USSR and the United States, the Allies were the countries that fought against Germany, Italy and Japan during World War II.

Axis: The Axis was made up of the countries that fought against the Allies during World War II. These included Germany, Italy and later Japan.

Battle of Britain: An air battle in the late summer and fall of 1940. Germany's Luftwaffe attempted, but failed, to gain control of British airspace and destroy the Royal Air Force (RAF), to prepare for an invasion of Britain by sea.

GLOSSARY

Bombing and Gunnery School: A BCATP school to train men to become air bombers or air gunners; training included air-firing practice.

Boston: An American-made twin-engine light bomber.

British Commonwealth Air Training Plan (BCATP): This program prepared some 130,000 aircrew to serve in World War II. Most of the training took place in Canada.

D-Day: The commonly used name for the Allied invasion of Normandy, which began June 6, 1944. The "D" doesn't stand for anything; it simply indicates the day on which a military operation will begin.

Distinguished Flying Cross (DFC): Awarded to British and Commonwealth officers for an act or acts of valour, courage or devotion to duty performed while flying in active operations against the enemy.

Distinguished Flying Medal (DFM): Awarded to non-commissioned officers (NCOs) and men for an act or acts of valour, courage or devotion to duty performed while flying in active operations against the enemy.

Elementary Flying Training School (EFTS): A BCATP school that gave future pilots basic flying training.

F-86 Sabre: A single-engine swept-wing (wings set at an angle to the fuselage) jet fighter. The Sabre was the first swept-wing jet flown by the RCAF.

Finger Four: The RAF name for a flying formation based on the German *Schwarm* (meaning "swarm" or "cluster") formation. A group of four planes would be positioned like the four fingers of the hand and could break into pairs in combat.

Flight: A flying subgroup (up to twelve planes) of a squadron.

Focke-Wolf 190: A German single-engine fighter plane, larger than a Messerschmitt 109.

Hurricane: A British-designed single-engine fighter plane.

Initial Training School (ITS): A BCATP school that determined whether recruits would become pilots, navigators, wireless operators, etc.

Junkers 88: A German twin-engine bomber; later in World War II, it was also used as a fighter plane.

Kittyhawk: An American-built fighter-bomber of World War II.

Luftwaffe: The German air force in World War II.

Manning Depot: A place that introduced men to RCAF training while they waited for openings in an Initial Training School.

Messerschmitt Komet: The only rocket-powered aircraft of World War II; it was introduced by the Germans late in World War II.

Messerschmitt 109: A German World War II fighter plane.

Messerschmitt 262: A German fighter plane that was the world's first operational turbojet aircraft; it was in combat only in the last year of the war.

NORAD: North American Aerospace (formerly Air) Defense Command; founded in 1958, it is a joint organization that provides surveillance and control of Canadian and American airspace.

Operational Training Unit (OTU): The final step in the BCATP, the OTU allowed airmen to prepare for combat flying. Most BCATP graduates received their OTU training in Britain.

Order of Canada: This is Canada's highest civilian honour; it recognizes outstanding achievement, dedication to the community and service to the nation.

RCAF: The Royal Canadian Air Force.

RAF: The Royal Air Force, Britain's air force.

Section: A subgroup of a flight.

Service Flying Training School (SFTS): A BCATP school where pilots learned advanced flying techniques, such as night flying and instrument flying.

Squadron: The basic Allied air force unit of twenty-four planes. Up to twelve planes (known as a flight) were airborne at one time.

Spitfire: A British-made World War II single-engine fighter plane.

Tempest: A British-made fighter plane introduced late in World War II. It was used to defend against V-1 rockets.

U-boats: German submarines (from *Unterseeboots*, meaning "undersea boats").

Vampire: A British-designed fighter plane; it was the first jet flown by the RCAF, starting in 1948.

V-1 Rocket: A German flying bomb introduced late in World War II; it was the first modern guided missile.

"Vic": A V-shaped flying formation, with the leader's plane in front and two more planes behind and to either side.

Wing: An organizational grouping of several Allied squadrons.

ACKNOWLEDGMENTS

Above all, I want to thank Stocky Edwards for his patience and good humour through many interviews and phone conversations. It was a privilege to be entrusted with his memories. Thanks to Stocky and Toni for their warmth and hospitality in Comox, and for the world's best oatmeal recipes. My old friend John Laidler was my indispensable point man in Comox, liaising with Stocky, scanning pictures and so on. Emile Francis shared vivid memories of Stocky as a young hockey player. Thanks also to John Chaput and Don MacEachern, for hockey facts and research leads; the staff of the RCAF Museum in Trenton, for James Edwards interview tapes; and Harold Johnstone, for providing me with two detailed accounts of the Desert War that I otherwise would not have seen. *Kittyhawk Pilot* and *Kittyhawks over the Sands*, by James F. Edwards and Michel Lavigne, are the definitive works

ACKNOWLEDGMENTS

on Stocky's exploits with 94 and 260 Squadrons, as well as much else about World War II in the air.

Once again, I want to express my gratitude to my insightful editor, Lynne Missen, as well as to Noelle Zitzer, Felicia Quon and Melanie Storoschuk of HarperCollins, for their professionalism and enthusiasm. Janice Weaver's copy editing improved every page.

Finally, I want to thank my husband, Eric Zweig, for his unflagging support and encouragement, for his uncanny research skills, and for coming up with the perfect title for the book.

PICTURE CREDITS

We gratefully acknowledge James "Stocky" Edwards for permission to reproduce the images within the text, except for the following:

The photo of the London Blitz, found on page 43, from the National Archives (UK).

The diagram of the Finger Four formation, found on page 55, drawn by William Band.

The photo of the Messerschmitt plane, found on page 61, used by permission from Harold Kindsvater.

The D-Day photo, found on page 104, from the National Archives of Canada (PA-137014), Gilbert Alexander Milne, photographer.

ARNOLD MACHTINGER

BARBARA HEHNER is the author of many children's books, including *The Tunnel King*; *The Spirit of Canada: Canada's Story in Legends, Fiction, Poems and Songs*; *Journey to Ellis Island*; and *First on the Moon*. She began writing over 20 years ago, entering into a partnership with David Suzuki. Together they wrote six children's science and activity books, starting with *Looking at Plants*. Barbara Hehner lives in Toronto with her family.

To receive updates on author events and information about Barbara Hehner, sign up at www.authortracker.ca.